PENGUIN BOOKS — GREAT FOOD

## Buffalo Cake and Indian Pudding

ALVIN WOOD CHASE (1817–1885) was born in Cayuga County, New York, and spent his early years peddling household wares and medicines along the Maumee River near Toledo, Ohio, where he also collected folk remedies. His first edition of *A Guide to Wealth! Over One Hundred Valuable Recipes for Saloons, Inn-Keepers, Grocers, Druggists, Merchants and Families Generally* was published in 1858, and by the 1863 edition the book contained over 800 recipes. In 1897 he published *Dr. Chase's Third, Last and Complete Receipt Book*. His books were great sellers, especially among pioneers and settlers who were eager to have a multi-purpose how-to guide to assist them in everyday life.

# Buffalo Cake and Indian Pudding

## DR A. W. CHASE

PENGUIN BOOKS

## PENGUIN BOOKS

Published by the Penguin Group
Penguin Group (USA) Inc., 375 Hudson Street, New York, New York 10014, U.S.A.
Penguin Group (Canada), 90 Eglinton Avenue East, Suite 700, Toronto, Ontario,
Canada M4P 2Y3 (a division of Pearson Penguin Canada Inc.)
Penguin Books Ltd, 80 Strand, London WC2R 0RL, England
Penguin Ireland, 25 St. Stephen's Green, Dublin 2, Ireland
(a division of Penguin Books Ltd)
Penguin Books Australia Ltd, 250 Camberwell Road, Camberwell, Victoria 3124,
Australia (a division of Pearson Australia Group Pty Ltd)
Penguin Books India Pvt Ltd, 11 Community Centre,
Panchsheel Park, New Delhi – 110 017, India
Penguin Group (NZ), 67 Apollo Drive, Rosedale, Auckland 0632, New Zealand
(a division of Pearson New Zealand Ltd)
Penguin Books (South Africa) (Pty) Ltd, 24 Sturdee Avenue,
Rosebank, Johannesburg 2196, South Africa

Penguin Books Ltd, Registered Offices: 80 Strand, London WC2R 0RL, England

*Dr Chase's Third, Last and Complete Receipt Book* first published 1887
This extract first published in Great Britain in Penguin Books 2011
First published in the USA by Viking Studio, a member of
Penguin Group (USA) Inc. 2011
1 3 5 7 9 10 8 6 4 2

All rights reserved

Printed in Great Britain by Clays Ltd, St Ives plc

Cover design based on a pattern from a Chochoti Pueblo jar, American School,
*c.* 1885. (Photograph copyright © Bridgeman Art Library.) Picture research
by Samantha Johnson. Lettering by Stephen Raw.

Without limiting the rights under copyright
reserved above, no part of this publication may be
reproduced, stored in or introduced into a retrieval system,
or transmitted, in any form or by any means (electronic, mechanical,
photocopying, recording or otherwise), without the prior
written permission of both the copyright owner and
the above publisher of this book.

The scanning, uploading, and distribution of this book via the Internet or
via any other means without the permission of the publisher is illegal and
punishable by law. Please purchase only authorized electronic editions and
do not participate in or encourage electronic piracy of copyrightable materials.
Your support of the author's rights is appreciated.

ISBN: 978–0–241–95633–5

www.penguin.com

Penguin Books is committed to a sustainable
future for our business, our readers and our
planet. This book is made from paper certified
by the Forest Stewardship Council.

# Contents

## CULINARY RECIPES

| | |
|---|---|
| Bread | 1 |
| Puddings | 13 |
| Pies | 27 |
| Cakes | 37 |
| Various Dishes | 68 |
| In Memoriam | 75 |

# Culinary Recipes

Bread, Puddings, Pies, Cakes . . . and
Various Dishes

## BREAD

*Remarks* – If the simple word 'bread' only, is spoken, it is always understood to mean white, or bread made from wheat flour. Other kinds always have a descriptive attachment, as Graham, Indian, brown, Boston brown, corn, etc. Two things are especially essential in good bread – lightness and sweetness. If bread is heavy – not light and porous – or if it is sour, it is only fit for the pigs. And it is important to know that good bread cannot be made out of poor flour. In the following these points are nicely explained, together with full and complete instructions in the three necessary processes of making good bread – making sponge, kneading, and baking.

**How to Make Good Bread** – A loaf of perfect bread, white, light, sweet, tender, and elastic, with a golden brown crust, is a proof of high civilization; and is so indispensable a basis of all good eating that the name 'lady,' or 'loaf-giver,' applied to the Saxon (English, as now understood, for England was overrun and conquered by the people of Saxony, in northern Germany, in an early day, so that now, to say a 'Saxon,' or of the Saxon race, refers to the English, descended from them, more often than to the people of Saxony itself – and especially Anglo-Saxon always means English) matron, may well be held in honor by wife or maiden. But do all the gracious ladies who preside in our country homes see such loaves set forth as daily bread?

Inexperienced housekeepers and amateur cooks will find it a good general rule to attempt at the beginning only a few things, and learn to do those perfectly. And these should be, not the elaborate dishes of special occasions, but the plain every-day things. Where can one better begin than with bread? The eager patronage of the over-crowded, carelessly served, high-priced Vienna bakery at the Centennial gave evidence that Americans appreciate good bread and good coffee, and had, perhaps, some effect in stimulating an effort for a better home supply. To make and to be able to teach others to make bread of this high character is an accomplishment worth at least as much practice as a *sonata* (a piece of music); and the work is excellent as a gymnastic exercise. With good digestion, honest personal pride, and the grateful admiration of the family circle as rewards, surely no girl or woman who aspires to responsibilities and joys of home, will shrink from the labor of learning to make bread.

The whole art and science of bread-making is no mean study. The *why*, as well as the *how*, should be aimed at, although exact knowledge or science, even in bread-making, is not so simple a matter as some might fancy. Varying conditions, even the temperature of the kitchen, work confusion in the phenomena of a batch of bread as surely as in the delicate experiments of a Tyndall or a Huxley. Fortunately, an exhaustive knowledge is not essential to practical success. Skillful manipulation will come with experience, and I have taught the actual art to a succession of uneducated cooks so that, with a little supervision, they satisfactorily supplied an exacting family. But the mistress, the house-mother, who must give intelligent direction, will not be satisfied without going to the root of the matter. Let her not rest upon her laurels without making sure that her table is constantly supplied with such delicious loaves of 'the staff of life' as, with the fragrant, highly-flavored butter of May or June, shall make a fit repast even for the good women whose hand have prepared them.

**Good Flour Essential** – The first requisite to good bread is good flour (and *sifted*, to enliven it and make it mix more readily). If the very best seems too expensive, make up the difference in cost by eating less cake. With really delicious bread you will do this naturally, and almost unconsciously.

**The Yeast, to Make** – In the country, where fresh yeast from breweries is out of the question, the first process must be making yeast; and it is well to begin there, and know every step of your way. The commercial yeast cakes must form a basis; from them it is easy to make the potato yeast, which is perhaps the simplest and best of several good forms of soft yeast. Dry yeast cake used directly will not make bread of the first quality. For the yeast, soak *three yeast cakes* in a cup of tepid water, while *six* or *eight* fair-sized potatoes are boiling. When they are perfectly soft, put the potatoes, with a quart of water in which they were boiled, through a colander, and add a teaspoonful of salt and two of sugar. When tepid, add the yeast cakes, rubbed with a spoon to a smooth paste, and place the whole in a stone jar, and keep the contents at blood heat for twelve hours, when a lively effervescence should have taken place. The yeast will be in perfect condition the next day, and will remain good for ten days or more if kept in a cool cellar in a closely covered jar.

**Setting the Sponge** – Many New England housekeepers make a great mistake in setting their sponge over night. One secret of good bread is that every stage of the process must be complete and rapid. Every moment of waiting means deterioration. At the precise moment *when the sponge is fully light* the bread should be kneaded, and the process of rising ought not to require more than *three hours* at most. Set your sponge, then, as early in the morning as you like, by taking in the bowl or basin kept for the purpose (and you will soon learn just how high in it the sponge should rise) two quarts of *sifted* flour. Make a hole in the middle with the stirring spoon; pour in half a pint of the soft yeast, first thoroughly stirring it from the bottom, then mixing with the flour; add tepid water, stirring constantly, until a smooth, stiff batter is formed, which stir and beat vigorously with the spoon for at least five minutes after it is perfectly mixed. Cover lightly, and set in a warm place until thoroughly light, almost foaming; but be sure not to delay kneading until it begins to subside.

**Kneading** – Sift the flour, say 6 qts., in a pan, make a hole in the middle, pour in the sponge; add a pinch of salt, and, dexterously mingling the flour with the soft sponge by the hand, gradually add a quart of warm milk or warm water, quickly incorporating the whole into a smooth, even mass. Cover the kneading-board with flour, place upon it the dough, which must not be soft enough to stick or stiff enough to make much resistance to pressure, and knead vigorously and long. Half an hour's energetic kneading is not too much for a family baking. By that time the bread should be elastic, free from stickiness, and disposed to rise in blisters. Cover with a soft bread-cloth folded to four thicknesses, and set it where a temperature of about blood-heat will be maintained.

In two hours it should have risen to fully twice its volume. Place it again upon the board; divide with the hands (which may be floured, or, better, buttered) a portion of the size which you wish for your loaves, remembering that it will rise again half as much more; lightly mold it into a smooth, shapely loaf, with as little handling as possible, and place in a well-greased pan. Set the loaves back in their warm corner for half an hour, when they should be very light and show signs of cracking. Bake at once in a hot oven, with a steady heat, from 45 minutes to 1 hour, according to the size of the loaves. Take immediately from the pans and wrap in soft, fresh linen until cold.

**Biscuit From Some of the Dough** – A portion of the dough will make a pan of delicious biscuits by adding a piece of butter as large as an egg to sufficient dough for a small loaf, mixing it lightly but thoroughly, and molding into small round balls, set a little distance apart in the pan. They will soon close up the space, and should rise to twice their first height. The swift, sure touch which makes the work easy, rapid, and confident, will come with practice; but the necessary practice may come only with patience and determination.

**To Make Bread Crust Soft and Delicate** – Take a cup of cream off the pan, and put it into your bread when you are about molding it, and it will cause the crust to be very soft and delicate.

*Remarks* – Knowing this to contain good sound sense, from the fact that I know the Vienna bread has a softer and more delicate crust than common bread, I mention it, believing that one reason, at least, for this is that the Vienna bread is made richer with milk than the common, as you will notice, by comparison. Bread should not be made too thin and soft, in kneading, nor too stiff and hard; but of such a consistence that when you press the doubled hand upon the mass of dough the depression will quickly rise up again to nearly its former shape. Let beginners be a little careful in all the foregoing points of instruction, and the author has no fears in guaranteeing a bread that they, even, shall not be ashamed of. If bread, or rather the sponge, becomes sour from being set over night (although it is conceded not to be best to set it over night), or from neglect to knead it at the right time (when just fully light), dissolve a tea-spoonful of soda (baking soda is always meant) in a little warm milk or water and work it in, which will correct it. If there is danger at any time, in baking, of burning, or over baking, cover the bread with thick brown paper, or a folded newapaper, until the loaf is done through; and if too hot at the bottom to endanger burning, put the oven grate, or a few nails or bits of iron, under the pan, which will prevent it from burning by the admission of air under it. By observing these points you are always safe.

**Rye and Indian Bread** – Take Indian meal, 2 cups, make in a thick batter with scalding water; when cool add a small cup of white bread sponge, a little sugar and salt, and a tea-spoonful of soda, dissolved. In this stir as much rye flour as is possible with a spoon; let it rise until it is very light; then work in with your hand as much more rye as you can, but do not knead it, as that will make it hard; put it in buttered bread tins, and let it rise for about 15 minutes; then bake it for 1½ hours, cooling the oven gradually for the last 20 minutes.

**Wheat and Indian Bread, Steamed** – Molasses, 1 cup; sour milk, 2 cups; soda, 2 tea-spoonfuls; flour and Indian meal, of each 1 pt. Directions – Beat well together, put into a buttered pan and steam 2 hours. – *Mrs. Carrie Case*.

*Remarks* – Perfectly reliable, for I have eaten it of her own make, and I shall never forget the 'jolly time' we had while eating it the first time.

**Brown, or Rye and Indian Bread, Steamed** – Indian meal, 1 qt.; rye flour, 1 pt.; stir these together and add sweet milk, 1 qt.; molasses, 1 cup; soda, 2 tea-spoonfuls; a little salt, and steam 4 hours.

**Brown, or Wheat and Indian, Baked** – Indian meal, 2 cups; stir into it ½ cup of cold water; stir well, and add 1 qt. of boiling water, allowing it to cool; then add 1 cup of molasses and a small soaked yeast cake; then stir in sifted flour to make it as thick as possible with the spoon and let rise over night; knead lightly in the morning, and bake slowly.

**Brown Bread, Rye and Indian, New England Style; or Steamed and Baked** – Rye flour, 4 cups; Indian meal (the yellow is generally used in making any of the brown breads), 3 cups; molasses, 1 small cup; cream tartar, ½ tea-spoonful; a little salt; mix very soft with sour milk or buttermilk; steam four hours, and then bake two.

**Boston Brown, Baked** – Take 4 cupfuls of Indian meal and 4 cupfuls of rye meal (not flour); sift through a coarse wire sieve; add 2 tea-spoonfuls of soda, a little salt, 1 cupful of molasses; 1 cupful of sour milk, and water sufficient to make a soft dough. Bake 4 hours in a moderately heated oven, or what would be better, 2 hours in a brick oven.

**Brown, or Minnesota Corn Bread, Steamed and Baked** – Corn meal and flour, each 2 cupfuls; sweet and sour milk, each 1 cupful; molasses, ½ cupful; salt and saleratus, or soda, each 1 tea-spoonful. Put into round tin cans, and steam 1 hour and bake ½ an hour.

**Brown, or Indian Bread, Baked for Tea** – Sour milk, 1 pt.; sweet milk, ½ pt.; molasses, 1 cupful; butter, ½ cupful; eggs, 3; saleratus, 2 tea-spoonfuls, or its equivalent in soda; salt, 1 large tea-spoonful; Indian meal, 1 qt.; flour, 1 pt. Mix all according to general rules, and bake in a deep basin, with oven same heat as for cake, for 1½ hours, or thereabouts.

**Indian Bread, Baked** – Take 2 qts. Indian meal, add 1 large spoonful of butter, 1 of sugar, a little salt; mix together; pour upon the whole 1 qt. of boiling water; then cool with cold water sufficiently to add ½ cupful of good yeast. Let it rise for 2 hours, then add wheat flour (if the dough is not thick enough) so as to give it the consistency of 'pound cake.' Put it into deep dishes, let it rise for 1 hour. Bake in a stove oven. You will find it delicious. – *Mrs. L. B. Arnold, Ithaca, N.Y.*

**Indian Bread, Extra, Steamed** – Buttermilk, sweet milk and Indian meal, each 3 cups; flour, 2 cups; soda, 2 tea-spoonfuls; salt, 1 tea-spoonful. Mix, put into a greased or buttered pan (as all should be), and steam 3 hours.

**Old-Fashioned Indian, or Corn Bread** – This is from Mrs. S. N. Ross, Sparta, O., in Toledo *Blade:* 'The recipe which I have is the nearest to the old Dutch-oven corn bread of anything that can now be baked: Two pt. cups of Indian meal, 1 pt. cup of flour, 2 pt. cups of sweet milk, 1 pt. cup of sour milk, ½ pt. cup of sugar, 1 tea-spoonful of salt, 1 tea-spoonful of soda. Mix, and bake slowly 1½ hours.'

**Corn Bread, Southern, Far-Famed** – The following re-cipes, obtained through the *Blade*, give you the different plans of making the celebrated 'Southern Corn Breads' and 'Southern Corn Dodgers,' and will be found very satisfactory, as well as a very healthful form of bread. The first is from the 'Old Lady' who always knows how to do things in the 'Household' line, while the second claims to be an improvement upon that, and the third, the latest style of corn dodger, *i.e.*, baked on tins or in a pan, while the old style or plan was to wrap them in corn husks, or paper, wet, and then bake them in the embers or upon the hot hearth. The 'Old Lady' says:

'Take 2 eggs, beat them well; add 1 pt. of water, and stir well; put in 1 tea-spoonful of salt, same of yeast powders, and add meal enough to make a batter that will pour out of the pan. Put a table-spoonful of lard into the baking pan, set it in the oven and let it get hot; pour the batter in it and bake a nice brown. I assure you you will never make any other kind after eating this.' – *Old Lady, Mobile, Ala.*

## Corn Bread, Southern, Improved – This writer says:

'In the *Blade* I saw a recipe for the "far-famed Southern Corn Bread." I was raised in the South, and have a few times eaten bread made in that way; but it is not the way we make our bread – and as I think there is an "excellence" about *ours*, I send you the recipe. Take 1 egg, a tea-spoonful of salt and 1 of soda (if the milk is very sour it will take more soda), and 1½ pts. buttermilk; then put in white corn meal enough to make a nice tolerably thick batter. It is very nice baked in a bread pan, but we like it best baked in gem irons, or muffin irons, as some people call them. Whatever it is baked in must be well greased and smoking hot when the batter is put in.

Serve while hot. Corn bread never was intended to be eaten cold.' – *Hawthorne, La Place, Ill.*

*Remarks* – It will be noticed that 'Hawthorne' calls for white corn meal. The Southern people raise the white corn only, or, at least, almost wholly so; and some people, even in the North, think it makes the best bread. It would be well, then, to give it a thorough trial in the North, and if it proves more valuable than the yellow, let it be raised especially for cooking purposes. I would say in regard to the idea that 'corn bread was never intended to be eaten cold,' I think it to be an error. I like it best warm, still I have eaten it many hundred times cold, and enjoyed it very much, although I believe it to be healthful while warm, and I know it is rather more palatable and pleasant warm; still, if there is any left over, I should by no means throw it away, but warm it up by steaming, else eat it cold, as preferred, or most convenient.

**White Corn Dodgers** – Take 1 pt. of Southern corn meal (white corn meal), and turn over it 1 pt. of boiling water, add a little salt and 1 egg well beaten up and stirred into the batter when nearly cold. Butter some sheets of tin and drop your cakes by the table-spoonful all over the pan. Bake for 25 minutes in a hot oven.

*Remarks* – Do not think for a moment, that because you may not have white corn meal, therefore, you can not make corn bread or corn dodgers, for you can; although the yellow meal may not be quite as nice, yet it does make excellent bread, as well as griddle cakes, too, by using a very little white or graham flour with it.

**Apple Bread, Pumpkin Bread, etc.** – A very light, pleasant bread is made in France by a mixture of apples and flour (meaning wheat flour, of course), in the proportion of one of apples to two of flour (say cups or pints, as you please). The usual quantity of yeast employed as in making common bread, and the yeast is beaten with the flour and warm pulp of the apples (dried) after they are boiled and mashed, and the dough is then considered 'set;' it is then allowed to rise from 8 to 12 hours, then baked in long loaves. Very little water is needed.

*Remarks* – This will make nice and very pleasant flavored as well as healthful bread, but I must caution against giving it too long a time to rise. 'Keep an eye on it,' and when properly risen make into loaves and bake, lest some one should go by the '8 to 12 hours.' Use judgment in all cases, and there will be but few failures. I have known my mother and my wife to use pumpkins in a similar manner, even with corn meal as well as flour, which gave a pleasant relish to the bread. And if I was a woman I should try peaches which had been peeled before drying, believing that I should get a still finer flavored bread. Not the sourest, but a medium tart apple or peach only should be used. I think the proportion of apple above given is greater than is generally used of pumpkin. About 1 cup to each loaf of bread would, in my opinion, be enough, instead of 1 of apple to 2 of flour or meal or rye and Indian, etc. It is used with either or all kinds of bread, when desired, except the Vienna.

## PUDDINGS

**PUDDINGS** – *General Remarks and Directions* – Puddings are much like cake, and require about the same manipulation (skillful hand-working), and much the same ingredients. Eggs should be well beaten, and usually the whites and yolks are beaten separately although not quite so essential; but if so beaten the yolks should be beaten into the sugar before creaming in the butter, then the whites, having been well beaten; saving the whites of a sufficient number, when desired, to frost the top of a pudding – latterly called a *méringue*, made by whipping the whites of three or four eggs to a froth, with a table-spoon of powdered sugar to each egg used, with a little lemon juice, or such other fruit juice, as orange, etc., or some of the flavoring extracts, as rose, cinnamon-waters, etc., as you have or prefer; the pudding, when just done, to be carefully drawn to the mouth of the oven and covered with the frosting, or *méringue*, and a few minutes more given to nicely brown it; then taken hot to the table – nothing, it seems to the author, is so out of place as to pretend to have a pudding, just baked, come to the table only luke-warm (half cold); for me, I tell them: 'Save this for me till tea-time, as I love cold pudding very much.' But, of course, I would not add: 'I dislike a half-cold one,' but I do dislike them 'all samee.' Bread puddings, or those made with corn-starch, rice, or fruits, require only a moderate oven to bake them; while butter or custard puddings require not only a quick oven, but should go into it as soon as all the ingredients

13

are mixed in with a final thorough beating, or stirring, and placed in the oven at once. The pudding-dish should always be well buttered, and, if to be a boiled pudding, the cloth must be first dipped into boiling hot water, then well floured on the outside. If boiled in a basin or mold, it must be buttered, and if a cloth is to be tied over it, it is to be treated the same as for boiling in a cloth; then when done, either way, dip into cold water, which will allow it to be emptied at once, without sticking, into a suitable dish to place upon the table; but always keep covered with the cloth or a napkin until placed upon the table, but there ought to be no delay in serving after it is emptied out of the cloth. It is usual to direct that 'puddings be tied loosely,' but you will see in the first receipt, that this plan is wrong, as it gives too much chance for water to get in and make them 'soggy.' Steam puddings often swell up and crack open – a sure sign of tightness. In boiling a pudding, remember this, the water must be boiling before the pudding is put in, and not allowed to slacken lest it becomes clammy or 'soggy,' as the sailor calls it in the first receipt. Keep the pudding also well covered all the time by pouring in boiling hot water, if needed, from time to time. To prevent the pudding from adhering or sticking to the kettle, cloth or dish, while boiling move it occasionally or else put a tin cover of some other dish into the bottom of the kettle, to make at least half an inch space from the kettle – the rim around the cover does this. To show the real value of the old English plum pudding, I take my first one from the New York *Times*, as related by a sailor – the second mate on a ship from New York to Liverpool – in which case, of course, even the half of the Christmas plum pudding saved (?) the ship and quickly brought all safely to their desired haven. Note well the instructions given in the receipt part of the item, as they will all be found correct and worthy to be followed, on land as well as on the sea. I take the item from the Detroit *Free Press*, but it originated with the *Times*, as credited above. It is as follows:

English Plum Pudding – It was about the stormiest voyage I ever see. We left the Hook on November 5, 1839, in a regular blow, and struck worse weather off the Banks (New Foundland), and it grew dirtier every mile we made. The old man was kind of gruff and anxious like, and wasn't easy to manage. This ain't no Christmas story, and ain't got no moral to it. I was second mate and knowed the captain pretty well, but he wasn't sociable, and the nearer we got to land according to our dead reckoning (for we hadn't been able to take an observation) the more cross-grained he got. I was eating my supper on the 24th, when the steward he comes in, and says he, 'Captain, plum pudding to-morrow, as usual, sir?' It wouldn't be polite in me to give what that captain replied, but the steward he didn't mind. All that night and next day, the 25th of December, it was a howling storm, and the captain he kept the deck. About 3 o'clock Christmas day dinner was ready, and a precious hard time it was to get that dinner from the galley to the cabin on account of the green seas that swept over the ship. The old man, after a bit, came down, and says he, 'Where's the puddin'?' The steward he come in just then as pale as a ghost, and says he showing an empty dish: 'Washed overboard, sir.' It ain't necessary to repeat what that there captain said. Kind of how it looked as if the old man had wanted to give himself

15

some heart with that pudding, and now there wasn't none. I disremember whether it wasn't a passenger as said 'that, providing we only reached port safe, in such a gale puddings was of no consequence.' I guess the old man most bit his head off for interfering with the ship's regulations. Just then the cook he came into the cabin with a dish in his hand, saying: 'There is another pudding. I halved 'em,' and he sot a good-sized pudding down on the table. Then the old man kind of unbent and went for that pudding and cut it in big hunks, helping the passenger last, with a kind of triumphant look. He hadn't swallowed more than a single bit than the first mate he comes running down, and says he: 'Lizard Light on the starboard bow, and weather brightening up.' 'How does she head?' 'East by north.' 'Then give her full three points more northerly, sir, and the Lord be praised.' And the captain, he swallowed his pudding in three gulps, and was on deck, just saying, 'I knowed the pudding would fetch it,' and he left us. We was in Liverpool three days after that, though a ship that started the day before us from New York was never heard of. This here is the receipt for that there pudding:

Take six ounces of suet, mind you skin it and cut it up fine. Just you use the same quantity of raisins, taking out the stones, and the same of currants: always wash your currants and dry them in a cloth. Have a stale loaf of bread, and crumble, say three ounces of it. You will want about the same of sifted flour. Break three eggs, yolks and all, but don't beat them much. Have a teaspoonful of ground cinnamon and grate half a nutmeg. Don't forget a teaspoonful of salt. You will require with all this a half pint of milk – we kept a cow on board of ship in those days – say to that four ounces of white sugar. In old days angelica root candied was used; it's gone out of fashion now. [Angelica grows all over the United States, as well as Europe, has a peculiar flavor, and was, at least, once believed to be a very valuable medicine, but used more, of late, merely for the agreeable flavor it imparts to other medicines. The root is of purplish color, and is to be sliced up and cooked in sugar, if 'candied,' as referred to above, the same as citron or lemon, etc., are done. King sets it down as 'aromatic, stimulant, carminative, diaphoretic, expectorant (this often used in cough or lung medicines), diuretic and emenagogue.' Used in flatulent colic and in heartburn. It is said to promote the menstrual discharges. In diseases of the Urinary organs, as calculi and passive dropsy, it is used as a diuretic in decoction with *uvaursi* and *eupatoriaum purpuseum* (queen of the meadow). DOSE – of the powder 30 to 60 grs.; of the decoction (tea), 2 to 4 ozs, 3 or 4 times a day. There are several species, or kinds, of it, any of which may be used medicinally as a substitute for other kinds.] Put that in – if you have it – not a big piece, and slice it thin. You can't do well without half an ounce of candied citron. Now mix all this up together, adding the milk last in which you put half a glass of brandy. Take a piece of linen, big enough to double over, put it in boiling water, squeeze out all the water, and flour it; turn out your mixture in that cloth, and tie it up tight; good cooks sew up their pudding bags. It can't be squeezed too much, for a loosely tied pudding is a soggy thing, because it won't cook dry. Put in 5 qts. of boiling water, and let it boil 6 hours steady, covering it up. Watch it, and if the water gives out, add more boiling water. This is a real English plum pudding, with no nonsense about it.

**Christmas Plum-Pudding, No. 6, Old Style** – Stone 1½ lbs. of raisins, wash, pick and dry ½ lb. of currants, mince fine ¾ lb. of suet, cut into thin slices ½ lb. of mixed peel (orange and lemon), and grate fine ¾ lb. of bread-crumbs. When all these dry ingredients are prepared; mix them well together, then moisten the mixture with 8 eggs, well beaten, and one wine-glass of brandy; stir well, that everything may be thoroughly blended, and press the pudding into a buttered mould; tie it down tightly with a floured cloth, and boil 6 hours. On Christmas day a sprig of holly is usually placed in the middle of the pudding, and about a wine-glass of brandy poured round it, which, at the moment of serving, is lighted, and the pudding thus brought to the table encircled in flames.

*Remarks* – With half-a-dozen plum-puddings none need go without a Christmas day, certainly. The only point that seems to me unreasonable is the long boiling, 8, or even 6 hours, which appears to be more than is needed. A circle of three ladies, to whom I referred the matter, gave it as their judgment that 3 hours would be sufficient. Let English people stick to the old custom, but Americans will find that from 3 to 4 hours will cook them perfectly. [See the Paradise Pudding below, which is only to be boiled 2 hours.] A wine-glass, at least, of brandy is almost universally put into the sauce upon Christmas occasions.

**Paradise Pudding** – Pare, core and mince 3 good-sized tart apples into small pieces, and mix them with ¼ lb. of bread-crumbs, 3 eggs, 3 ozs. of currants, the rind of one-half lemon, ½ wine-glass of brandy, salt, and grated nutmeg to taste. Put the pudding into a buttered mould, tie it down with a cloth, boil for 2 hours, and serve with sweet sauce.

*Remarks* – These fancy names, no doubt, are calculated to convey the idea that the article is to be very nice. The author would prefer to see more common names used, but he takes them as he finds them, so long as the article itself, like this pudding, is really nice. 'Angels' Food' has been recently advertised; so these dear creatures will not have to 'live on air' much longer.

**Sauce for Puddings – The Author's Favorite** – The best sauce to suit me is made by using rich cream with plenty of pulverized sugar, so the spoon will fetch it up from the bottom of the 'boat,' or bowls, at every dip – and I like to dip deep every time; milk does very well, but it is well-known that it is not so rich as cream; but half-and-half does excellently. Use any flavoring you please; grated nutmeg is the most common with cream sauce.

**Orange Pudding** – Peel and slice 4 large oranges, lay them in your pudding dish and sprinkle over them 1 cup of sugar. Beat the yolks of 3 eggs, ½ cup of sugar, 2 table-spoonfuls of corn starch, and pour into a quart of boiling milk; let this boil and thicken; then let it cool a little, before pouring it over the oranges. Beat the whites of the eggs and pour over the top. Set it in the oven to brown slightly. – *Mrs. R. McK. of Jackson, Mich., in Farm and Fireside*.

**Pop-Corn Pudding** – Sweet milk and pop-corn, each 3 pts. (each kernel must be popped white, and not a bit scorched); eggs, 2; salt, ½ teaspoonful. Bake ½ hour.
*Sauce for Same* – Sweetened cream or milk.

**Chestnut Pudding** – Peel off the shells, cover the kernels with water, and boil till their skins readily peel off. Then pound them in a mortar, and to every cup of chestnuts add 3 cups of chopped apple, 1 of chopped raisins, ½ cup of sugar, and 1 qt. of water. Mix thoroughly, and bake until the apple is tender – about ½ hour. Serve cold with sweet sauce.

*Remarks* – Whoever loves chestnuts (and who does not) will like the flavor of this pudding. Take out a chestnut from the boiling water, and drop it into cold water a moment, and if the dark skin will rub off with the thumb and finger (which is called blanching), they have boiled enough.

**Apple, Peach, or Other Fruit Pudding-Pie, or Pie-Pudding, No. 2, Yankee Style** – Sweet milk, 1 cup; 1 egg; butter, 1 table-spoonful, heaping; baking powder, 1 tea-spoonful; flour, 1 cup, or sufficient to make rather a thick batter ('batter' means like cake – better to handle with a spoon, or to pour out); a little salt; tart, juicy apples to half fill an earthen pudding-dish. DIRECTIONS – Stir the baking powder into the sifted flour; melt the butter, beat the egg and stir all well together; having pared and sliced the apples or peaches, buttered the dish and laid in the fruit to only half fill it, dip the batter over the fruit to wholly cover it, as with a crust; the dish should not be quite full, lest as it rises it runs over in baking. Bake in a moderate oven to a nice brown, to be done just 'at the nick of time' for dinner. Turn it bottom up upon a pie-plate, and grate over nutmeg or sprinkle on some powdered cinnamon or other spices, as preferred; then sprinkle freely of nice white sugar over all and serve with sweetened cream or rich milk, well sweetened. Peaches, pears, strawberries, raspberries, blackberries, etc., in their season, work equally as well as apples. – *Mrs. Sarah A. Earley, Mt. Pleasant, Iowa.*

*Remarks* – This plan avoids the soggy and indigestible bottom crust of pie; and it matters not whether you call it pie or pudding, it eats equally well, even cold, with plenty of sugar and milk, having the cream stirred in.


**Hunters' Pudding, Boiled – Will Keep for Months –** Flour, suet finely chopped, raisins chopped, and English currants, each, 1 lb.; sugar, ¼ lb.; the outer rind of a lemon, grated; 6 berries of pimento (all-spice) finely powdered; salt, ¼ tea-spoonful; when well mixed add 4 well beaten eggs, a ½ pt. of brandy, and 1 or 2 table-spoonfuls of milk to reduce it to a thick batter; boil in a cloth 9 hours, and serve with brandy sauce. This pudding may be kept for 6 months after boiling, if closely tied up; it will be required to be boiled 1 hour when it is to be used. – *Farm and Fireside.*

*Remarks* – This, for hunters going out upon a long expedition, would be a very desirable relish to take along. There is not a doubt as to its keeping qualities, as it contains no fermentive principles; and the fruit and brandy are both anti-ferments, while the long boiling is also done to kill any possible tendency to fermentation. I should, however, boil it in a tin can, having a suitable tight-fitting cover, if intended for long keeping, on the principle of air-tight canning, as well as to be safe from insects, and convenience in carrying. Do not think, however, but what it would be very nice for present use with only 4 or 5 hours' boiling, using the sauce freely, as it is made so dry for the purpose of long keeping.

**St. James' Stale Bread Pudding** – Grate a stale loaf of bread (*i.e.*, 2 or 3 days old) into crumbs; pour over them 1 pt. of boiling milk; let stand 1 hour; then beat to a pulp; then beat, sugar, 1½ cups, to a cream with 4 eggs, and butter, 2 table-spoonfuls; grate in the yellow of a lemon, and a bit of nutmeg, and a pinch of cinnamon, if liked; beat all well together, and pour into a pudding dish lined with nice puff paste, and bake about 1 hour. The juice of the lemon to be used in making whatever sauce you prefer, as there are many already given.

*Remarks* – The author feels very sure you will ask St. James to call again. Bread, buttered well on each side, may be substituted for the puff paste to line the dish.

**Bread Pudding, Aunt Rachel's** – 'Aunt Rachel,' in the *Rural New Yorker*, says: 'A pudding may be made of small pieces of bread, if the family taste does not rebel. [I never see the family taste rebel against so good a pudding.] The bread should be broken fine, covered with milk, and set on the stove where it is not too hot, until it becomes soft. Remove and stir in a table-spoonful of sugar, 1 of butter, a small tea-spoonful of salt, also a pinch of cinnamon, or allspice, and, if liked, ½ cup of chopped or cut raisins, or dried raspberries. When cool enough, stir in an egg, well beaten, and bake 1 hour in a moderate oven. To be eaten with cream and sugar, or pudding-sauce, as preferred.'

*Remarks* – This is like what my wife used to make, except she used to put the raisins in whole, to which I should never object; nor did I, as above remarked, 'ever see the family taste rebel against it.'

'Aunt Rachel' adds: 'I knew a lady who kept all the broken pieces of bread in a bag, that was hung where they would dry and not mold, and she had the material for a pudding always at hand. The price of flour and cost of living would determine whether such economies would pay.' It would pay, unless it may be for farmers, who raise their own wheat and have fowls to feed the broken pieces of bread to.

**Blackberry Pudding, Baked or Boiled, and a Jelly, or Jam, as Sauce for Same, and a Cordial for the Children** – A writer in the *Western Rural* gives the following very nice ways of using this delicious fruit in its season. For the pudding: Take nicely ripe blackberries and sweet milk, each 3 pts.; eggs, well beaten, 5; sugar, 1 cup; a little salt; yeast powder (the author would say baking powder, as it acts quicker), 2 tea-spoonfuls, and flour to make a suitable batter to handle with a spoon, if to be baked; and as stiff as can be worked if to be boiled. To be eaten with any sauce, or the following jelly or jam:

*For the Jelly* – Place perfectly ripe blackberries in a porcelain kettle with just water enough to keep from burning, stirring often, over a slow fire, until thoroughly scalded; then strain or drain through a jelly-bag, the berries having been well mashed by the stirring in scalding – twice through, if necessary to make it clear; – measure, and put the juice on the stove and boil briskly 10 minutes;

then add equal measures of nice white sugar, and continue to boil until a bit of it dropped into a glass of very cold water sinks at once to the bottom, instead of dissolving much in the water, when it is done, and makes a splendid sauce for the pudding.

*For the Jam* – To each pound of the berries put, for present use, half as much light brown sugar, and boil to thoroughly cook the fruit, and use as sauce for the pudding; but for longer keeping, for winter use, use berries and sugar equal weights, and cook carefully 1 hour, stirring constantly to avoid burning. It is a cheap and excellent preserve, of which the children are very fond; and it is valuable for the younger ones having the least tendency to bowel complaints, and may be given half-and-half with the cordial, flavored highly with cinnamon, of which most children are very fond.

*For the Cordial* – Take the very ripest blackberries, mash them in a suitable tub or pail, pressing out the juice through a stout piece of muslin; and to each quart put 1 lb. of best loaf or lump sugar, also in a porcelain kettle, pouring on the juice, and as soon as softened place on the stove and boil to a thin jelly only; and when cold add brandy, ½ pt. to each pound of sugar used. If this is to be given to very young children, the jelly may be used in place of the jam, in equal parts, thus avoiding the seeds. For a child of 2 to 5 years, put 2 or 3 table-spoonfuls of each into a glass with a tea-spoonful of essence or extract of cinnamon, mixing thoroughly, and giving a tea- to a table-spoonful of it as often as they like, or every half hour until relieved.

*Remarks* – This shows the great value and variety of ways in which the blackberry may be used.

**Whortle (Huckle) Berry Pudding, Boiled** – Eggs, 4, well beaten; sweet milk, 1 pt.; salt, 1 tea-spoonful; nicely assorted and fully ripe whortle-berries, 3 pts; stir all well together, then stir in sifted flour to make a stiff batter, tie tightly in a properly prepared pudding-cloth, mold or dish, and boil or steam 2 hours. To be served with any sweet sauce, or sugar and butter creamed.

**Sweet Potato Pudding** – A writer in the *Blade Household* gives us the following ingredients: Buy sweet potatoes, 2 lbs. (they are sold by the pound now almost wholly); brown sugar, ½ lb.; butter, ⅓ lb.; cream, 1 gill (¼ pt.); 1 grated nutmeg; a small piece of lemon peel; eggs, 4; flour, 1 table-spoonful. DIRECTIONS – Boil the potatoes well and mash thoroughly, passing it through a colander; and while it is yet warm mix in sugar and butter; beat the eggs and mix in when cool, with the flour, grated lemon peel, nutmeg, etc., very thoroughly; butter the pan and bake 25 minutes in a moderately hot oven. May be eaten with wine sauce. I would say yes, or any other sauce, and still be good, very good.

**Indian Pudding, No. 1, Baked** – This pudding was made at the Cataract House, Niagara Falls, by Mrs. Polk, for thirty-six successive seasons: One quart of milk put on to boil; 1 cup of meal, stirred up with about a cup of cold milk; a piece of butter, about the size of an egg, stirred into the hot milk, and let boil; beat 6 eggs, or less, with 1 cup of powdered sugar, and add a tea-spoonful of ginger and nutmeg; then stir the whole together, and have it thick enough to pour into the dish, buttered. Bake in a quick oven.

*Sauce for Same* – One cup powdered sugar; ½ cup butter, beaten to a cream. Flavor with nutmeg and a little wine or brandy, to taste.

*Remarks* – Myself and family spent several days at the above hotel, in 1874, where we were so well pleased with this pudding – as has always been my custom, in my travels, if I found some particularly nice dish upon the table – I made an effort (through the waiter) to obtain the recipe, and, by 'oiling the machinery,' at both ends of the route – paying waiter and cook – I succeeded. I have given it word for word as dictated by Mrs. Polk (colored), who was highly gratified because we were so much pleased with her pudding, assuring us she 'had made it in the same house for thirty-six seasons, without missing one.' The family having made it many times since, I can, therefore, assure every one 'it is genuine,' and very nice indeed. Coarse meal is considered better than fine for baked puddings; and if the milk is rich by stirring in the cream so much the better. They are made without eggs, molasses taking the place of sugar.

## PIES

**PIES – The Pie of Our Fathers – Minced Pie –** *General Remarks* – Any pie, to be good, ought to have a light and flaky crust, or 'pastry,' as more recently called, and the filling should be put in sufficiently thick to remove all suspicion of stinginess on the part of the maker, both of which points are most eloquently brought out in the following communication of Jennie June's, to the *Baltimore American*, written more particularly as a defence of the minced pie, or 'the pie of our fathers,' as she calls it, against which so much has not only been said, but written. It is so rich in thought, eloquent in argument, and correct in its principles of instruction, it is worthy of a perusal, at least on Christmas occasions, by all lovers of minced pie, who have not 'abused their stomachs,' as she puts it, 'until they have become dyspeptics.' Such persons may feel grieved that they cannot allow themselves to indulge in this luxury any more, but they should have been reasonable in an earlier day, then they would not feel a necessity for complaint. Some writers claim that minced pies are bad, only, when eaten just before retiring. Such a plan with any food, to be made a habit of, is bad. The stomach needs, and must have rest, as well as the body, or it will sooner or later make a complaint, never to be forgotten. She says:

'I feel moved to say a word in defense of not only the pie in general, but the pie in particular – the symbolic *mince pie*, which the people who have abused their stomachs until they have become dyspeptics unite in abusing. The mince pie is a very ancient institution, and the only pie that has religious

27

significance. The hollow crust represents the manger in which the Savior was laid; its rich interior, the good things brought by the wise men as offerings and laid at His feet. A good mince pie is not only better for digestion than a poor one but it has a representative character of its own – it symbolizes our love and devotion to the divine principle to which the Christmas festival is consecrated. Mince pies should be prepared with a due sense of their character and importance. They should not be eaten often; but they should be well-made of fine and abundant materials, and, when served, received with due regard and given the place of honor. Thin layers of impoverished mince, inclosed in flat, ceramic (hard, like earthenware) crust, are *not* mince pies; they are the small-souled housekeeper's substitute for the genuine article. The true mince pie is made in a brown or yellow earthen platter, is filled an *inch thick* with a juicy, aromatic compound, whose fragrance rises like incense the moment heat is applied to it, and it comes out the golden brown of a russet which has been kissed by the sun. No common or nerveless hand should be allowed to prepare or mix the ingredients for this sum of all pastry. Every separate article should be cut, cleansed, chopped, sifted, with strong but reverent touch, and the blending should be effected with the sweetest piece of the apples, reduced by boiling with the sirup of the maple and sacramental wine. Thus the spices of the East, the woods of the North, the sweetness of the South, and the fruit of the West is laid under tribute, and the result, if properly compounded, is a pie that deserves the esteem in which it was held in ancient times, and does credit to the skill of our foremothers, who brought it to its present state of perfection and to the good judgment of our forefathers, who appreciated and ate it. Let us defend and sustain one of our time-honored institutions against the attack of a weak and effete generation, which, having demoralized itself by indulgence in many more obnoxious pleasures of the table, makes the "pie" the scapegoat, and especially the "mince pie," which, when deserving of its name, is a revelation of culinary art – a kitchen symphony – deserving the respect and consideration of all who understand and appreciate a combination and growth which has achieved the highest possible result.'

**Pastry, or Crust, No. 1, for Minced and all other Pies –** As it is of the utmost importance to have a light and flaky crust for minced pies, as well as all others, I will give two or three plans of making. The first is the celebrated Soyer's Receipt given by 'Shirly Dare,' in the *Blade Household;* and, although it is some labor to make it, it will pay to follow it whenever a very nice, flaky crust is desirable. It is as follows:

'To every quart of sifted flour allow the yolk of 1 egg, the juice of 1 lemon, 1 saltspoonful of salt, and 1 lb. of fresh butter. Make a hole in the flour, in which put the beaten egg, the lemon and salt, and mix the whole with *ice water* (*very cold* water will do) into a soft paste. Roll it out, put the butter, which should have all the buttermilk thoroughly worked out of it, on the paste, and fold the edges over so as to cover it. Roll it out to the thickness of a quarter of an inch; fold over one-third and roll, fold over the other third and roll, always rolling one way. Place it with the ends toward you, repeat the turns and rolls as before twice. Flour a baking sheet, put the paste in it on ice or in some very cool place half an hour, roll twice more as before; chill again for a quarter of an hour; give it two more rolls and it is ready for use.

'This is very rich paste, and may be made with *half* the quantity of butter only, chopped fine in the flour, rolled and chilled, forming a very light puff paste that will rise an inch, and be flaky throughout.'

*Remarks* – The object of chilling the pastry, by putting it upon ice or into a cold place, is to keep the butter cold, so it shall not be absorbed into the crust, but keep its buttery form, which makes it flaky, by keeping the dough in layers, while the many foldings and rolling out makes them thin, like flakes of snow. But it is only in *hot* weather that this chilling becomes necessary, and not then, unless you desire it to be flaky. In making pie by the last paragraph above, using only ½ lb. of butter to 1 qt. of flour, for common use, the lemon juice, and egg too, may be left out, using the salt however. Still the yolk of an egg gives some richness, but more especially a richness of *color*. And even *half* lard, or 'drippings' may be used, as indicated at the close of the 1st receipt below, and be good enough for all common purposes, using the egg, or not, as you choose.

It has always seemed to me, however, that pie-crust ought to have soda or baking-bowder in it to make it light; and to be certain about it, I have just called on one of our best bakers in the city and asked him about it. He tells me that some bakers keep flour, sifted with baking-powder or soda, ready for use; and, in making crust, they take one-fourth of the amount of flour to be used from that having the baking-powder or soda in it, to make the crust rise a little, and help to prevent any soggyness from using a juicy pie-mixture; but he says it depends more upon the heat on the bottom, or rather from the want of a proper heat at the bottom of many stoves. With the uniform heat of the bottom of a baker's brick-oven they have no trouble, generally, in baking the bottom crust so it is done, and hence not soggy. To do this in a stove-oven, move the pie occasionally to another part of the oven, where the heat has not been absorbed or used up in heating the plate or tin – in other words, see that the bottom of the oven is kept as hot as it ought to be, and you have no soggy or under-done crusts. Pies, not to be eaten the day they are baked, should be baked harder than those for immediate use, to prevent the absorption of the juice of the pie or dampness from the air.

**Minced Pies, No. 1** – Boil a fresh beef's tongue (or very nice tender beef in equal amount, about 3 lbs), remove the skin and roots (any remains of the wind-pipe, blood vessels, etc.) and chop it very fine, when cold; add 1 lb of chopped suet; 2 lbs of stoned raisins; 2 lbs of English currants; 2 lbs of citron, cut in fine pieces; 6 cloves, powdered (½ teaspoonful powdered cloves); 2 teaspoonsful of cinnamon; ½ teaspoonful of powdered mace; 1 pt. of brandy; 1 pt. of wine, or cider; 2 lbs of sugar; mix well and put into a stone jar and cover well. This will keep some time. When making the pies, chop some tart apples very fine, and to 1 lb of the prepared meat put 2 bowls of the apple: add more sugar if taste requires it, and sweet cider to make the pies juicy, but not thin; mix and warm the ingredients before putting into pie plates. Always bake with an upper and under crust, made as follows:

**Crust** – Lard, butter and water, each 1 cup; flour, 4 cups.

*Remarks* – To which I would add, the yolk of an egg and a little salt. As a general thing, I do not think so much brandy and wine are used, and although I do not object to eating, occasionally, of such a pie, yet, as many persons do, they can leave them out, substituting boiled cider – 3 to 1 – in the place of the brandy or wine; or pure alcohol, ½ pt., would be as strong in spirit, and cost less than half as much, while the difference in taste would not be observed. Each person can now suit themselves and be alone responsible. I will guarantee this much, however, no one will be led into habits of drink from the amount of spirit they will get in a piece of pie thus made – possibly one-fourth of a teaspoonful. Nearly all receipts for minced pies contain wine or brandy; they can be used or left out, as any one shall choose, by using the cider more freely.

**Pumpkin Pie** – Stewed pumpkin, 1 heaping pint; 6 eggs; flour, 6 table-spoonfuls; butter, size of an egg; sugar, 1½ cups; cinnamon, 2 level tea-spoonfuls; ginger, ½ tea-spoonful; ½ a grated nutmeg. DIRECTIONS – Rub the pumpkin through a colander, adding the butter, sugar and spices, and make hot, then the beaten eggs and flour; mix smoothly together, and while hot put into the dish, having a thick crust to receive it, and bake in a moderate oven. – *Henry Crane, Frost House, Eaton Rapids, Mich.*

*Remarks* – This makes a thick, salvy pie, very nice. If

fearful of a soggy crust, bake it before putting in the pie mixture. If a pint of milk was added, it would be more like the old-fashioned pumpkin-custard pie, softer and not quite so rich, unless an additional egg or two, with an extra cup of sugar is put in. If milk is plenty, and pumpkin scarce, take this latter plan.

**Pumpkin and Squash, Best for Pies, Prepared by Baking –** Ruth H. Armstrong, in the *Housekeeper*, says: If all housekeepers who make pumpkin pies knew how much better and easier it is to bake the pumpkin first, they would no longer worry over cutting up and peeling it, but just cut it in halves, take out the seeds, lay it in the oven and bake until soft, when it can be scraped out and used as usual, and is so much better for not having water in it. Winter squash makes a much richer pie when treated in the same way.

**Squash Pie, Very Rich –** Stew a medium sized crook-necked (or other equally rich) squash, and rub the soft part through a colander, as for the pumpkin pie, above; butter, ½ lb.; cream and milk, each 1 pt., or milk with the cream stirred in, 1 qt.; sugar, 2 cups; 1 dozen eggs well beaten; salt, mace, nutmeg and cinnamon, 1 teaspoonful each, or to taste.

*Remarks* – Of course the mixing and baking, the same as for the pumpkin pie above; and if less is needed for the family keep the same proportions as in that also. I think good squash makes a richer pie than pumpkin, while some persons claim the reverse, and call for an egg or two extra. If a poor quality is used, this would be so;

but crook-necked, or Hubbard, are much nicer than pumpkin, both in quality and flavor, and I like this pie much the best, but can get along very nicely even with a good rich pumpkin pie.

**Potato Custard Pie** – Nicely mashed potatoes, 1½ cups; sugar, 2 cups; milk, 1 qt.; eggs, 5; a little salt, and any flavoring desired. DIRECTIONS – Beat the eggs well, mix all, and dip into the pans made ready with the usual paste, or crust, and bake the same as custard pie.

**Sweet Potato Pie** – Sweet potatoes make an equally nice pie, for all who, like myself, are fond of them, treated the same as their Irish brethren above.

*Remarks* – Sweet potatoes make a richer pie than the common potato, as much so as good squash makes a pie richer, in quality and flavor, than common pumpkin; but as the Irish potato keeps the best, a pie can be made of them, after the sweet ones are out of season.

**Grandmother's Apple Pie** – Line a deep pie-plate with plain paste. Pare sour apples – greenings are best – and cut in very thin slices. Allow 1 cup of sugar and a quarter of a grated nutmeg mixed with it. Fill the pie-dish heaping full of the sliced apple, sprinkling the sugar between the layers. It will require not less than six good-sized apples. Wet the edges of the pie with cold water; lay on the cover and press down securely that no juice may escape. Bake three-quarters of an hour, or even less if the apples become tender. It is important that the apples should be well done, but not over-done. No pie in which the apples are stewed beforehand can be compared with this in flavor.

**Rabbit Pie, Fricasseed and Roast** – Cut up the rabbit, remove the breast bone and bone the legs. Put the rabbit, a few slices of ham, a few force-meat balls, and 3 hard-boiled eggs, by turns, in layers, and season each with pepper, salt, 2 blades of pounded mace, and ½ teaspoonful of grated nutmeg. Pour in ½ pt. water, cover with crust, and bake in a well-heated oven for 1½ hours. When done, pour in at the top, through the middle of the crust, a little good gravy, which may be made of the breast and leg bones, flavored with onion, herbs and spices.

*Fricasseed* – Rabbits, which are in the best condition in midwinter, may be fricasseed like chicken in white or brown sauce.

*To Roast* – Stuff with a dressing made of bread-crumbs, chopped salt pork, thyme, onion, and pepper and salt, sew up, rub over with a little butter, or pin on it a few slices of salt pork, and a little water in the pan, and baste often. Serve with mashed potatoes and currant jelly.

**Oyster Pie** – Small oysters, 1½ qts.; cracker crumbs, 1 cup; salt and pepper to suit. DIRECTIONS – Drain the oysters in a colander, and throw away the juice, unless you wish to cook it, seasoning properly and eating it as 'soup,' with some crackers; there will be juice enough from the oysters. Line the sides of a deep buttered pie-dish with a crust made as for the chicken and other meat pies above; put a layer of the oysters, salt and pepper to suit; then a light sprinkling of the cracker crumbs, and so fill the dish; put over the top some bits of butter to season nicely, and cover with a crust; bake in a quick oven. As soon as the pastry is done the oysters will be cooked also.

*Remarks* – By using the juice the pie is made too mushy, or soggy.

Escaloped Oysters, or Oyster Pie With Crackers – Oysters, 1½ qts.; crackers, sufficient; pepper, salt and a little mace. DIRECTIONS – Drain the oysters as above; butter the dish and put a layer of the oysters over the bottom; then, the crackers being thin, butter one side lightly, and place a row of them around the dish in place of a crust; season the oysters, each layer as you go along, then sprinkle on some cracker-crumbs, else split crackers, buttered, does nicely in place of crumbs, and so fill the dish, or until the oysters are all in, putting another tier of crackers up the side, if needed, as you fill up to the top of the first tier, and cover the top with a layer of buttered crackers, putting on the butter pretty freely on the top crackers, which melts down into the dish and makes a crispy cover or crust, without the trouble of making pastry.

*Remarks* – If this new plan is done carefully you will be pleased with the result. If not, you can take the old crusty, mushy way again; but I know you will not.

# CAKES

**CAKE-MAKING, BAKING, ETC.** – *General Remarks and Explanations* – To make good cake every article used must be good, of its kind – flour, sugar, or molasses, butter or lard, eggs, spices, or flavoring extracts, fruit, cream of tartar and soda, or saleratus, or baking-powder, milk, etc.

But to save repeating the explanation with every cake receipt given (many of which must be very similar, if not absolutely the same), I will make such an explanation in connection with each of the articles mentioned as entering into cake-mixtures that persons can soon familiarize themselves with, all that is necessary, to a full and complete understanding of the whole subject, without the repetition referred to.

Flour – It being understood, then, that all the articles, or material used in making cake shall be good, I need only say: The flour will be the better if put into the oven and thoroughly dried – stirring a few times while drying – then sifted; and if cream of tartar with soda, or baking-powder are to be used, they – or the one to be used – should be stirred into the flour before sifting.

Sugar and Butter – Use your own judgment at to whether white or light brown sugar may be used. For common purposes the light brown will do very well; but if a delicate cake, for any particular occasion, is to be made, use pure white sugar and very nice butter. If sugar is at all lumpy, crush by rolling, then the sugar and butter should always be creamed together, *i.e.*, beaten together until they are completely blended into a mass, much the appearance of cream, hence the word 'creamed' has been appropriately applied. And this creaming of the butter and sugar is a very important part of cake-making; for, by this process, the oiliness and consequent indigestibility of the butter is overcome, the cake rises brighter, and is much more healthy and digestible than by rubbing the butter into the flour, which has heretofore been the more usual custom.

In cold weather it may be necessary to place the butter in a warm place a short time to soften – not to melt – to enable the creaming to be properly done.

**Lard and Drippings** – Neither lard nor drippings are as good as butter, but, for family use, half the amount may be very satisfactorily put in the place of half of the butter named.

**Molasses** – When molasses is used the cake will scorch quickly if the oven is too hot; hence for these, and for cakes having fruit in them, bake in a moderate oven, especially such as fruit loaf-cakes, they being generally thick, require a longer time for baking. Then, if there is danger of burning the top, in any case, cover with brown paper, until nearly done.

**Eggs** – Eggs must be fresh and well-beaten; and it is claimed that all cakes are better if the yolks and whites are beaten separately. This may be true, to a certain extent, but my wife who has made cake for me (or seen that it was done as she desired) for over forty years, claims, and I have no doubt of the fact, that the difference, for general use, is not sufficient to pay for the extra trouble; while, for nice cake, for special occasions, it may be best to beat separately.

**Spices** are always to be ground, or very finely pulverized, where the old fashioned mortar is still in use.

**Flavoring Extracts,** kept by dealers may be used, or those made by receipts given in this work, which will be found under proper headings, using only sufficient to obtain a fair flavor of the fruit represented.

**Fruit** requires care in selection, or purchase, and also in its preparation for use.

**Raisins** need to be looked over to free them from any remaining stems, and from small gravel-stones, which are often found among them, then washed, drained, dried and floured, and used whole, or they may be seeded and chopped after washing and draining, then rubbed – 'dredged' – with flour, which largely prevents them from settling to the bottom of a cake or pudding.

**English Currants** require picking carefully to free them from gravel, dirt, etc., and several careful washings, for the want of proper care in curing. They also require drying and flouring, the same as raisins, for the same reason.

**Home-dried Fruit** – Currants, raspberries, blackberries, whortle ('huckle') berries, etc., may be substituted for foreign fruit very satisfactorily when desired, or when they are plenty.

**Citron**, when used, is to be 'shred,' *i.e.*, cut into long narrow strips, or chopped, as preferred. If chopped, however, leave it the size of peas, so that one eating the cake can tell what it is without too close scrutiny.

**Almonds** are to be blanched, *i.e.*, boiling water is to be poured upon them and allowed to stand until the thin skin will rub off easily, then chopped as citron, or pounded finely in rose water – preferably chopped.

**Cream of Tartar and Soda** are always to be stirred into the flour before it is sifted, the same as baking powder. The proportions in using should always be two of the first to one of the latter. They are usually kept in separate boxes and mixed when used, by taking out 2 teaspoons of the cream of tartar to 1 of the bi-carbonate of soda (baking soda), but they may be purchased in quantities of ½ lb. of the cream of tartar to ¼ lb. of the soda (or in these proportions) and all mixed at once, if dry, and kept in an air-tight box in a dry place, and thus you have always ready for use a better baking powder than you can buy.

**Saleratus**, when used, is to be dissolved in a little hot water, or in a little of the milk, by rolling finely on the table or moulding-board before putting into the cup to dissolve. After the same is dissolved, add it to the cake mixture.

**Soda**, when used alone, is to be treated the same as saleratus.

**Baking Powder** should always be mixed into the flour, the same as cream of tartar and soda, before the flour is sifted.

**Milk** is always to be sweet when baking powder, or cream of tatar with soda are to be used. Sour milk or buttermilk when soda, or saleratus only are to be used.

**Making Up or Putting Cake Together** – The eggs being properly beaten, the flour sifted, the sugar and butter creamed, everything to be used being placed within reach, little by little add the milk to the creamed sugar and butter, stirring constantly, then the yolks of the eggs (when beaten separately), after which the sifted flour, having the proper amount of baking powder, or cream of tartar and soda in it, and then the fruit (if fruit is to be used), spices or flavoring extracts; but, now, if saleratus is being used, it is to be dissolved and stirred in, and lastly the beaten whites of the eggs, stirring but little after these are added; but the more thorough the stirring together, previous to putting in the whites, the better.

**Baking – Heat of the Oven, etc.** – To bake cake nicely, the heat of the oven should be uniform throughout the whole time of baking; and for light, thin cakes (and that covers nearly all, except those having fruit in them) a quick oven is required, so that by the time the cake is properly raised the baking shall commence; for if the heat is not uniform throughout the baking there will be a soggy streak shown in the cake, because if the cooking slackens much the cake begins to 'fall,' and although the heat may be again raised, yet what has settled together will not rise again; while if you get too great a heat simply cover the cake with brown paper to prevent burning the top, and partly close the damper to prevent too much heat from passing under the bottom; but the oven door must not be left open in cake baking, or else the cake will 'fall,' the same as if the heat had fallen off for want of fuel. Avoid, as much as possible, also, the moving of cake after it is placed in the oven and has began to rise, as the motion may cause the escape of gas, leaving the cake heavy, and especially is this important with cake containing grated or desiccated cocoanut.

**Pans** – Pans should always be well buttered, except for thick, or loaf cake, which requires the bottom of the pan to be covered with a buttered piece of white paper, buttering the sides, unless deemed safest to paper the sides also, especially if the cake is a thick fruit cake, and in this case the top must be covered with brown paper until nearly done.

**To Know When a Cake is Done,** pierce it with a clean broom splint. If it comes out free of the cake mixture it is done; but a few minutes more had better be given it than to have it at all under done.

**Hints and Suggestions** – If attention is given to the above explanations and a moderate degree of experience is brought to bear upon the following recipes, I have no fears of a failure; and those who have not been instructed as they should have been by their mothers, or those having the care of them in their minority, and now find it necessary to make cake for themselves and their husbands, must begin with the cookies, and other smaller and plainer cakes, lest a failure should too greatly discourage them; and should they fail a few times, take the mottoes, 'don't give up the ship,' but 'try, try again,' and ultimate success must follow.

**Special Explanations** – If any special explanations are needed, they will be given in connection with the recipe.

**Lastly – Keeping Cakes** – Keep cakes in the cook-room until cool; then wrap and place them in boxes with covers to exclude the air. Jelly cakes, however, had best not be removed from the plates upon which they have been built up, but need to be wrapped and placed in boxes, the same as others, which insures their moisture much longer than if not put away in boxes. Fried cakes, cookies, etc., after becoming cool, may be put into stone jars, and a cloth of several thicknesses be put upon them, pressing it down around the edge, then another cloth over the top of the jar, with a plate upon it will keep them sufficiently moist. It is not best to make large amounts of them at a time. Bread needs the same care to keep it nicely moist.

**Table of Explanations and Comparative Weights and Measures** – When white sugar is called for, 'A,' or first-class coffee sugar is intended.

The cup intended to be used is the common sized tea-cup, but if larger amounts are needed for large families, double the number, or use the larger coffee-cup.

1 lb. white sugar equals about 2½ cups; 1 lb. butter, 2 cups; 1 lb. lard, 2 cups; 1 lb. wheat flour, 3½ cups; 1 lb. graham, 3½ cups; 1 lb. Indian meal, 3½ cups.

**Icing, Boiled, for Cakes** – Powdered sugar, (and this is the right kind to use for all Icings), 2 cups; boiling water, 1 gill; whites of 2 eggs; flavoring to suit. DIRECTIONS – Pour the boiling water upon the sugar in a suitable dish, upon the stove, and boil until it readily creams, then pour this hot upon the beaten whites, and beat till cool, when it is ready to use, the cake being cold, or, at least, cool; add vanilla, lemon, or orange extract, rose or cinnamon water, or essence, a teaspoonful to a tablespoonful, to suit, and dip upon the cake; smoothing, if necessary, with a knife wet in cold water.

**Icing, Boiled, that will not Break** – White sugar, 1 cup; white of 1 egg; put water enough into the sugar to dissolve it; put it on the fire and let it boil till it will 'hair.' Beat the white of the egg to a stiff froth; pour the heated sugar on to the froth and stir briskly until cool enough to stay on the cake. The icing should not be applied until the cake is nearly or quite cold. This quantity will frost the tops of two common sized cakes. – *Godey's Lady's Book*.

**Boiled Icing – Quick to Harden** – To 1 cupful sugar, take 1 egg. Put sugar in pan and a little water over it, and let boil 20 minutes. Beat white of egg stiff and gradually beat boiling sugar into egg. Flavor. Apply to cake quickly, as it soon becomes hard.

**Icing, Old and Confectioner's Plan, or Without Boiling –** Icing or frosting for cakes was formerly done by beating the whites of eggs to a stiff froth, then beating in white sugar till stiff, or as hard as desired; but if it is not desired to boil it, as above, a better plan is to take the white of 1 egg for each medium-sized cake, and at the rate of ¼ lb. of powdered sugar for each egg to be used; and first, throw in some of the sugar, then begin to beat, and, from time to time, throw in more of the sugar, continuing the beating until the sugar is all in, and the icing of a smooth and firm consistence – nearly or about half an hour will be required: The piece of a lemon or an orange, or any of the extracts, may be used to flavor, allowing sugar extra to absorb it.

*Remarks* – If beaten together as above, it hardens on a cake quicker than if the eggs were beaten, as of old, before the sugar was added; and if made as thick and as hard as it ought to be with the sugar, one coat will suffice; while in the old way it almost always required two. If in a hurry to have the cake ready, this may be set two or three minutes in a moderate oven to harden.

**Icing to Color Different Shades –** Any icing may be colored, if desired, a yellow with lemon or orange, and pink with strawberries or cranberries. Grate the yellow of a lemon or orange, squeeze some of the juice upon the gratings, put into a stout muslin and press out the coloring into the icing. Strawberries and cranberries are to be pressed in the same way, or their syrups used. If considerable is used, add powdered sugar to make them thick before stirring in.

**Icing Chocolate for Cakes** Flavored chocolate, 4 ozs.; whites of 2 eggs; powdered sugar, 20 tea-spoonfuls; corn starch, 4 tea-spoonfuls; extract of vanilla, 2 tea-spoonfuls. DIRECTIONS – Beat the eggs and add the sugar and corn starch, stirring together; then, having grated the chocolate before you began the other work, add it and beat to a smooth paste; then spread it upon the cake, the top layer as smoothly as possible, and place the cake in the oven a moment, turning it around, and the icing will become nice and glossy.

**Icing, Almond** – Blanched almonds, ½ lb. (for two ordinary cakes), rosewater, sufficient. DIRECTIONS – Rub the almonds to a smooth paste (in a mortar) by adding a little rosewater from time to time to moisten sufficient only to form the paste; and then mix with any of the icings having no other flavor.

**Icing With Gelatine** – More recently some cooks have been using gelatine in making icings. Where no eggs are to be had it will make a good substitute. For each cake, soak gelatine, 1 tea-spoonful, in cold water, 1 table-spoonful, till soft, or about ½ hour; then pour upon it hot water, 2 table-spoonsful, stir to perfectly dissolve it; then stir in, while warm, pulverized sugar, 1 cup, continuing to stir until perfectly smooth, and spread upon the cake.

CAKES – Martha's Cake – Remarks – As my wife's name is Martha, I trust I shall be excused for beginning the cake list of my 'Third and Last Receipt Book' with her favorite, especially as it is plain and not expensive, and by little changes, and flavoring, such a variety may be made out of it, as loaf cake, jelly cake, etc. Sugar, 2 cups; butter, 1 cup; 6 eggs; flour, 2 cups; sweet milk, ½ cup; cream of tartar, 2 tea-spoonfuls; soda, 1 tea-spoonful. DIRECTIONS – Familiarize yourself with the general remarks and explanations, at the head of this subject, then you will be able to make any ordinary cake – the articles, and proportions, only being mentioned. I only mention here the different ways this may be flavored, baked, etc.

This may be baked in a loaf, or in jelly cake tins (shallow pans) and, when cold, laid up with fruit jelly spread between the layers, and you may ice the top, or not, as you choose – sometimes with – sometimes without. Sometimes flavor with the juice and grated yellow of a lemon, again with an orange, or the extracts of one or the other, and again without either, being plain. And thus you can have a cake differing from the leopard's skin in this – its spots may be changed, and that as often as you like, giving a great variety of cake without change of composition, except in flavoring, icing, etc., or in not flavoring, or not icing, baking in loaf, or for jelly cake, or by baking in patty pans, as you choose, or as occasion may call for. Mrs. Chase occasionally ices them when baked in the little pans, especially so if the icing is being made for large cakes, at the same baking.

Watermelon Cake – I. White sugar, 2 cups; butter and

sweet milk, each ⅔ cup; whites of 5 eggs; flour, 3 cups; baking powder, 1 tea-spoonful. DIRECTIONS – Beat the eggs, sugar, butter and milk together; put the baking powder into the flour before sifting it in, and mix.

II. Red sugar (kept by confectioners), 1 cup; butter and sweet milk, each ½ cup; flour, 2 cups; baking powder, 1 tea-spoonful; whites of five eggs; raisins (nice large ones), ½ lb. DIRECTIONS – Beat together in the same order as the first, cut the raisins into halves, the longest way, and mix in last; then put some of the first into the pan, hollowing it in the center to receive all of the second or red part, if it is sufficiently stiff to allow it, piling it up in the round form as neatly as possible, to represent the red core of the melon; then cover with the balance of the white, so you have a white outside and a red core, like a watermelon, if neatly done.

**Watermelon Cake, No. 2** – *White Part:* White sugar, 2 cups; butter, 1 cup; sweet milk, 1 cup; flour, 3½ cups; whites of 8 eggs; cream of tartar, 2 tea-spoonfuls; soda, 1 tea-spoonful; dissolve the soda in a little warm water; sift cream of tartar in flour; mix.

*Red Part:* – Red sugar, 1 cup; butter, ½ cup; sweet milk, ⅓ cup; flour, 2 cups; whites of 4 eggs; cream of tartar, 1 tea-spoonful; soda, ½ tea-spoonful; raisins, 1 cup; mix. Be careful to keep the red part around the tube of the cake-dish; the white part outside; best to have two persons fill in, one the red and the other the white, going around the tube till full. – *Mrs. S. O. Johnson, in Inter Ocean.*

**Chocolate Jelly Cake** – Butter, ½ cup; sugar, 2 cups; flour, 3 cups; milk, 1 cup; 4 eggs; baking powder, 1 teaspoonful.

*Jelly* – Milk, 1 pt.; grated chocolate and sugar, each 1 cup; corn starch, 1 table-spoonful. DIRECTIONS – Cream the butter and sugar, eggs and milk, as usual (in the order here named); then sift in the flour and baking powder and bake in jelly cake tins. For the jelly: Bring the milk to a boil and stir in the grated chocolate and sugar, and, having rubbed the corn starch smooth in a little cold water, stir it in and boil until it forms a smooth jelly, or paste, as some call it; when a little cool put between the layers.

*Remarks* – In boiling milk it is safest to set the tin containing it into a larger pan containing a little water, which removes the danger of burning – otherwise, it requires constant watching and stirring. Allow me to say that this is my favorite chocolate cake, as it has no other flavoring, while it seems that many of the recipes call for vanilla or lemon or orange, etc.; but for me, give me a single flavor only in any cake. But it may be vanilla to-day and the next day lemon, then orange, and then chocolate; but a mixture of flavors only leaves one to wonder what the cook had been trying to imitate; but persons can suit themselves. A recipe is no sign that that flavor must be used. If you have not got what is called for, but have some other; or if you prefer some other flavor, the cake will be just as nice if you accommodate yourself to the circumstances or to your preferences. There is another point, also, which calls for an explanation: If you have fruit jellies on hand, they may sometimes be used in laying up any of these 'jelly cakes,' instead of those which are called for in the recipe. This also extends the varieties which may be made.

**Lady Fingers, as Made in India** – Sugar, 1 lb.; 8 eggs; flour, 1 lb. DIRECTIONS – Sift sugar and flour; beat the yolks separately, then beat with the sugar for 20 minutes; then beat in also the beaten whites, then, slowly, the flour, and drop upon white paper, long, to resemble the finger; dust sugar over them and bake in a hot oven. – *Indian Domestic Economy and Cooking.*

*Remarks* – These will be found equal in delicacy to a true 'lady's finger,' even with an engagement-ring upon it. I should say moderate oven, lest they melt, if too hot, in baking.

**Love Knots for Tea** – Little cakes folded over in the form of love knots are nice for tea. Flour, 5 cups; sugar, 2 cups; butter, 1 cup; a piece of lard the size of an egg; 2 eggs; sweet milk, 3 table-spoonfuls; soda, ½ tea-spoonful; a grated nutmeg, if liked, or as much cinnamon. DIRECTIONS – Sift the soda in the flour, then rub in the butter, lard and sugar, and then the beaten eggs, milk and spices, if any are used; roll thin and cut in strips an inch wide and 5 or 6 long, and lap across in a true love knot. Bake in a quick oven. *Ann Arbor Register.*

**National Cake** – White part – Cream together 1 cup white sugar and ½ cup of butter, then add ½ cup of sweet milk, the beaten whites of 4 eggs; ½ cup of corn starch, 1 cup of flour into which has been mixed 1 tea-spoonful of cream tartar and ½ tea-spoonful of soda. Flavor with lemon extract.

Blue part – Cream together 1 cup of blue sugar and ½ cup of butter, then add ½ cup of sweet milk, the beaten whites of 4 eggs and 2 cups of flour, in which mix 1 tea-spoonful of cream of tartar and ½ tea-spoonful of soda. No flavor.

Red part – Cream together 1 cup of red sugar and ½ cup of butter, then add ½ cup of sweet milk, the beaten whites of 4 eggs and 2 cups of flour, in which mix ½ tea-spoonful of cream of tartar and ½ tea-spoonful of soda. No flavor. Place in a bake pan, first the red, then the white, and last the blue. Bake in a moderate oven.

**Kansas Puffs** – One cup of sugar, ½ cup of butter, ½ cup of molasses, 1 cup of sour milk, 1 tea-spoonful of soda, 1 cup of chopped raisins, and 1 cup of currants. Flavor with cloves and cinnamon. Make a little stiffer than you would cake and bake in little gem pans. – *Ella J. Shirley, Larned, Ks.*

*Remarks* – Following our National colors, or red, white and blue, it is proper to give one of black and white, or the Union Jack (perhaps red and white would have been better, but we take them as we find them), for the Prince of Wales, by Miss E. R. Bruckman, of Tioga, Ill., in *Blade:*

**Prince of Wales Cake** – Black part – One cup of brown sugar, ½ cup each of butter and sour milk, 2 cups of flour, 1 cup of chopped raisins, 1 tea-spoonful of soda dissolved in warm water, 1 table-spoonful of molasses, the yolks of 3 eggs, 1 tea-spoonful each of cloves and nutmeg.

White part – One cup of flour, ½ cup each of corn starch, sweet milk and butter, 1 cup of granulated sugar, 2 tea-spoonfuls of baking powder, the whites of 3 eggs. Bake all in 4 layers. Put together with icing, a black, then a white, alternating.

**Ginger Snaps, Evangeline's** – This lady says: Somebody wanted a ginger snap recipe that would stay hard, and not get soft. One cup of butter, 1 cup of lard, 1 cup of brown sugar, 1 pt. of molasses, 1 table-spoonful of ginger, 1 cup of sour milk, 2 tea-spoonfuls of soda, 1 pt. of flour – use more, if needed. Melt lard and butter together, stir in the ginger, sugar and molasses; dissolve the soda in the milk; stir all together, put in the flour, roll out thin, cut and bake in a quick oven.

*Remarks* – If made sufficiently stiff, properly baked, allowed to get cold, then kept from the air, they will keep hard a very long time.

**Ginger Snaps** – Here is the way they make them in the Old Bay State (Massachusetts), and they consider them very excellent: Molasses, 1 cup; butter, 2 table-spoonfuls; ginger, 1 table-spoonful; saleratus, 1 tea-spoonful; flour. DIRECTIONS – Boil the molasses and stir in the butter, ginger and saleratus, rolled fine; and stir the flour in while hot; roll out thin, cut and bake.

**Ginger Snaps** – Sugar, 2 cups; 2 eggs; fried meat gravy, 1 cup; cider vinegar, 1 table-spoonful; ginger, 1 table-spoonful; soda, 1 large tea-spoonful; flour enough to roll; bake in a quick oven. Mrs. R. S. Armstrong is responsible for this.

**Ginger Snaps** – I will give you another from the 'Indiana Dutch Girl,' of Tillmore, Ind.: Lard or butter, 1 cup; New Orleans molasses, 1 cup; ginger, 1 table-spoonful; soda, 1 heaping tea-spoonful; flour enough to make a stiff dough; roll quite thin, cut with cake cutter and bake quick.

**Gingerbread, Soft** – Molasses, 3 cups; butter or lard, 1 cup; sour milk, 1 cup; 4 eggs; ginger, 2 table-spoonfuls; soda, 1 table-spoonful; flour, 7 cups. DIRECTIONS – Stir butter, sugar, molasses, and ginger together; then the milk and eggs well beaten; then the soda dissolved in a little hot water; then the flour.

*Remarks* – This writer to the *Blade* 'Household' only gives the name 'Jessie,' but assures her friends that 'I know this to be good, for I have used it over twelve years,' but the reading of it satisfied me it was good, hence I give it a place. Having given my whole life to the observation and test of practical items of a general character, I know as quick as I read a recipe whether it is reliable or not. At least, for several years past, I have tested but very few recipes which proved a failure; while, in my earlier experience, the failures were frequent. Such I now throw aside on their first reading.

**Gingerbread, Poor Man's** – Molasses, 1 cup; sugar, ½ cup; 1 egg; buttermilk, ⅔ cup; lard or butter, 1 table-spoonful; ginger, 1 table-spoonful; cinnamon, 1 tea-spoonful;

soda, 1 tea-spoonful; flour, 2 cups. 'A. Y. E.,' of O'Brien, Iowa, says of it: 'Good and very cheap. [See, also, 'Poor Man's Cake.']

**Ginger Cakes, or Bread** – 'Mrs. S. E. H.,' of Circleville, O., gives the *Blade* 'Household' the following, which I give in her own words: 'I give a good ginger cake recipe – one that has taken the premium at our county fair for the last five years: One pt. best Orleans molasses, 1 pt. of sour buttermilk, 1 large table-spoonful of ginger, 1 of lard, 1 of soda; dissolve the soda in the buttermilk; flour enough to make soft as you can handle, the softer the better. Turn on the bread-board, roll, cut into cakes, and bake in a quick oven. Try this. If you prefer it baked in pans, add 2 eggs, well beaten, and mix as other cake. A small lump of alum, dissolved, improves the cake.'

*Remarks* – Most people object to the use of alum in baking powders; then why not objectionable to use it here? I think it is not at all necessary; but if it is used, 'a small lump' is too indefinite. I would say not more than half to a tea-spoonful, at most. If pulverized, it dissolves quicker, using a little hot water.

**Boston Cream Cakes** – Water, 2½ cups; flour, 2 cups; butter, 1 cup; and 5 eggs. Boil the butter and water together; stir in the flour while boiling; after it is cool add the eggs well beaten. Put a large spoonful in muffin rings, and bake 20 minutes in a hot oven.

The cream for them is made this way: Put over the fire 1 cup of milk, add not quite a cup of sugar; 1 egg, mixed with 3 tea-spoonfuls of corn starch and 1 table-spoonful of butter. When cool add vanilla to the taste; boil a few moments only. Open the cakes and fill them with the cream. They are easily made, and are delicious.

**White Mountain Cake** – Sugar, 2 cups; butter, 1 cup; flour, 3 cups; sweet milk, ½ cup; whites of 10 eggs, beaten very stiff (or the whole of 5 eggs, if the shade from the yolks is no objection); cream of tartar, 2 tea-spoonfuls; soda, 1 tea-spoonful. DIRECTIONS – Bake in 3 deep jelly tins, or 6 thin layers. If iced, take the whites of 4 eggs; white powdered sugar, 2 table-spoonfuls; flavor to taste, if desired.

**White Mountain Cake, Iced** – Granulated sugar, 3 cups; butter, 1 cup; 5 eggs; sweet milk, 1 cup; flour, 3 cups; cream of tartar, 2 tea-spoonfuls; soda, 1 tea-spoonful; salt, 1 pinch. DIRECTIONS – Beat the butter, sugar, and yolks of the eggs to a cream; mix soda in the milk and the cream of tartar in the flour; add the whites just before the flour. Bake in jelly cake tins, browning a little.

*In Place of Jelly* – Take the whites of 2 eggs, a little water, and the proper amount of powdered sugar, beat together and with a knife spread over the top of each cake. Grate a fresh cocoanut and mix it with more sugar, and sprinkle it over the cakes; then lay-up, finishing the top the same.

*Remarks* – Especially applicable for use upon occasions when ice cream is to be served.

**Delicate Cake** – Flour, 3 cups; sugar, 2 cups; butter, ½ cup; sweet milk, ¾ cup, and 1 tea-spoonful of cream of tartar (or ¾ cup of sour cream), ½ tea-spoonful of soda. Beat well, then add the whites of 6 eggs beaten to a stiff froth, flour to taste.

*Remarks* – This is in the words of the 'Belle' of Libertyville, Iowa, and will be found delicate as belles in general.

**Jumbles** – Mrs. Phœbe Jane Rankin, of Illinois, gives the following recipe for a very nice jumble: Sugar, 2 cups; lard, 1 cup; beat to a cream, then add 2 eggs; sweet milk, 1 cup; soda, 1 tea-spoonful; cream of tartar, ½ tea-spoonful; then stir in flour till about as stiff as pound cake; put plenty of flour on the board; dip out the dough with a spoon; flour your rolling pin well; roll to about ¼ inch thick; sprinkle sugar over the top; cut out and bake in a quick oven; when done set on edge to cool; the softer they are rolled out the better they will be. Add a little lemon extract if you like.

**Apple Fritters** – Prepare the batter as for fritters, having washed, and sliced the apples, crosswise, and if you have a corer the core should have been taken out. Have the lard boiling hot. Drop the slices into the batter and see that every part is well covered; fry until brown, then turn and fry until done.

*Remarks* – These instructions are from Miss Arabell, of Knox City, Mo. I say Miss because, as she gives no 'sir' name, I take it for granted she had not found the 'sir.' I will guarantee the fritters, however, to be found nice.

**Mrs. Chase's Sponge Cake** – Sugar, 1 cup; 4 eggs; sweet milk, 3 table-spoonfuls; flour, 2 cups; baking powder,

2 tea-spoonfuls; salt, 1 pinch; orange or lemon extract (home-made), 2 tea-spoonfuls. DIRECTIONS – Beat the eggs, then beat in the sugar, add the milk, salt and flavor; and, having mixed the baking powder into the flour, sift it in, beat all together and bake in a quick oven.

*Remarks* – This will make 2 cakes if baked in the round tin, or 1 in the square. I have eaten of this many times with great satisfaction, and expect the same in eating of the one which, I am just informed, is ready for tea. Yet I give several others to meet all circumstances and desires. Sponge cake is credited with being the most healthful of any form of cake, for the reason that, as a general thing, no butter or other shortening is used, although of late, as will be seen below, some people are beginning to introduce them; but, for myself, I am very fond of one of the above, coming warm from the oven at tea-time, having some very nice butter to eat with it. Those who are dyspeptic had better forgo this luxury. My next is from 'Fern Leaves,' of Oswego county, N. Y., who told the *Blade* 'Household' that it would make 'roll jelly cake,' 'cup cake,' or 'plain cake.' It is as follows:

**Sponge Cake** – Sugar, 1 cup; flour, 1 cup; 3 eggs; water, 2 table-spoonfuls; baking powder, 2 tea-spoonfuls; salt and spice to taste.

The following is from somebody's lady friend, as the result of long experience: 'Flour, 1 cup; sugar, 1 cup; baking powder, 1 heaping tea-spoonful; cold water, 3 table-spoonfuls; flavor with lemon or vanilla. DIRECTIONS – Beat the whites and yolks separately, and add the water the last thing before baking.

**Butter Sponge Cake** – Butter, 1 cup; sugar, 2 cups; flour, 1½ cups; 6 eggs; cream of tartar, 1 tea-spoonful; soda, ½ tea-spoonful. DIRECTIONS – No special directions given, except to dissolve the soda in a table-spoonful of the milk, and mix the cream of tartar evenly with the flour, which is in accordance with my general directions.

*Remarks* – But as this recipe shows how a farmer's wife, of White Church, Kansas, makes sponge cake, I thought I would give her directions in full. It will be noticed that this cake is rich in eggs and butter; but if the Kansas farmers can not afford it I do not know who can.

**Charity Cake** – Sugar, 1 cup; butter the size of an egg; 1 egg; stir to a cream; add sweet milk, 1 cup; flour, 2 cups; cream of tartar, 2 tea-spoonfuls; soda, 1 tea-spoonful. – *Emily A. Hammond.*

*Remarks* – No other place so appropriate for a poor man's cake, as to let it follow charity cake, for who needs charity any more than a poor man is likely to.

**Poor Man's Cake** – One cup of sugar, 1 cup of milk, 1 table-spoonful of butter, 1 tea-spoonful cream of tartar, ½ tea-spoonful of soda dissolved in the milk, 1 egg, a little cinnamon, and flour to make it as stiff as pound cake.

**Potato Cake** – 'S. A. M.' (Sam), of Mogadore, O., claims this to be a new kind of cake. She says: Mashed potatoes, 1 cup; sugar, 1 cup; risings, 1 cup; ⅔ cup of shortening, and 3 eggs. DIRECTIONS – Stir well together about 5 o'clock P.M., and at bedtime stir all the flour in the mixture you can with a big spoon; keep in a warm place, and in the morning put it in gem dishes and let rise again. Bake in a slow oven, and you will have a cake that children and invalids can eat without harm.

**Buffalo Cake** – Sugar, 1 cup; butter, melted, 1 table-spoonful; 1 egg, beaten to a froth; soda, 1 tea-spoonful, dissolved in sweet milk, ⅔ cup; cream of tartar, 2 tea-spoonfuls; flour to make so it will pour on tins. Bake like jelly cake, and put custard or jelly between.

*Remarks* – Mrs. J. A. Heister, of Denver, Col., says: 'It is cheap and good enough for any one.' And I cannot account for the name, unless it is because the Denver people take it with them when they go out to hunt buffalo.

**Buckeye Cake** – Sugar, ¾ lb.; butter, ½ lb.; 6 eggs, well beaten; sweet milk, ½ pt.; 1 lb. of 'prepared' flour; flavor with vanilla. Good for Ohio people, where they use this kind of flour.

**Boston Cake** – Sugar, 1 cup; milk, 1 cup; butter, 1 table-spoonful; 1 egg; flour, 2½ cups; cream of tartar, 2 tea-spoonfuls; soda, 1 tea-spoonful; flavor with lemon or nutmeg. Nutmeg is their favorite; so much so, some of them have been accused of making wooden ones.

**Rock Cakes, To Make** – Break 6 eggs into a dish, and beat till very light; then add powdered sugar, 1 lb. (2½ cups), and mix well; then dredge in gradually flour, ½ lb. (1¾ cups), and English currants, ¼ to ½ lb., which have been nicely washed and dried. Mix all well together; then put on to a baking tin (size to suit) with a fork, to make them look as rough as you can. Bake in a moderate oven, about half an hour. When cool store them in a box and keep them in a dry place, and they will last as long as you keep them in the box; but if placed on the table at meal times they will not keep a great while.

**Aunt Lucy's Spice Cake** – Sugar, 2 cups; butter, ⅔ cup; 2 eggs; butter milk, 1 cup; soda, 1 tea-spoonful; cloves, 1 tea-spoonful; cinnamon, 1 table-spoonful; ½ of a nutmeg; 'rising flour,' 1 cup, or to make thick.

*Remarks* – Who ever knew a cake-making aunt that did not make a good cake? This will make a nice cake, however, even if common flour is used, as the soda will make it light.

**Pork Cake** – Fat salt pork, 1 lb.; strong coffee, 1 pt.; brown sugar, 4 cups; stoned raisins, 1 lb.; citron or English currants, ½ lb.; flour, 9 cups; soda, 1 table-spoonful; 1 nutmeg and 1 table-spoonful of cinnamon. DIRECTIONS – The pork is to be weighed free of rind and chopped very fine; then pour the coffee, boiling hot, upon it and set on the stove a few minutes before adding any of the other ingredients. The spices are all to be ground, and if citron is used, it is to be finely chopped. The raisins and other fruit are to be dredged with flour to prevent settling. Fit a piece of white paper to the bottom of the pan or pans and cover the top with paper also, to prevent burning. Bake in a moderate oven until a splinter can be thrust into it and pulled out without the cake sticking to it. – *Mrs. Carrie Case, Toledo, O.*

*Remarks* – This will be very palatable, and will keep as long as you will allow. It is excellent.

**Mother's Strawberry Shortcake** – I believe the Household and the editor will agree with me in thinking Puck never ate any strawberry shortcake. We are 50 years old, but don't we remember, as well as if it was but yesterday, the dear, delightful ones made by mother in our childhood, and don't we know just how they were made, too; we heard her tell so many times, as every one wanted her recipe. She made them as follows: Sour cream, 1 cup; cream of tartar, 1 tea-spoonful; soda, ⅔ tea-spoonful, with flour to make a suitable dough to roll ½ an inch thick, baked nicely; split open and spread each piece with the sweetest, freshest butter; then pour on to one of the halves, not 6 or 7 gritty, mussy berries, but 2 whole cups of those large, luscious ones from the south side of the garden; put on the other half for a cover, and pour over sweetened cream when eaten. – *Aunt Lulu, Red Willow, Neb*.

*Remarks* – The author loves all these aunts, because they know how it is done; but he would love them better if they were not ashamed of their real names. This is about as my own mother used to make them, so I know it will prove good and worthy to be followed by all who have the nice 'sour cream.' But good rich milk with soda – no cream of tartar – will do very nicely. Of course, any berries, fresh or canned, at all suitable for a short cake, ripe, nice peaches, or even a nice, thick custard, may take the place of strawberries when they are not plenty, or for the sake of variety. See the remarks also following 'Pumpkin Shortcake,' below.

**Pumpkin Shortcake, With Graham Flour** – 'Stewed and strained pumpkin or squash, "C" oatmeal porridge and water, each 1 cup. Beat these up together, and then stir in 3 cups of graham flour. Mix thoroughly, spread ½ an inch thick on a baking-tin, and bake half an hour in a good oven. Cover for 10 minutes, and serve warm or cold.'

*Remarks* – Our readers will see by the quotation marks (' ') that this is not my own, nor do I know who to credit it to. But I have given it for the sake of a few explanations, or remarks, which, I think, will be for the general good; and first, you will see that a porridge is called for made from 'C' oatmeal; what does the 'C' mean here? It means the grade of fineness of the meal, as known to dealers, the same as 'A' coffee sugar means the best – 'C' coffee sugar is not quite so good. While with the oatmeal it means not quite so coarse a meal as 'A' would be. For Scotch cake the finest kind is used, and, I should think, would be the best to make into a porridge. Second, some persons never use oatmeal porridge; then, unless people will use a little of good common sense, they, or persons living where they cannot get oatmeal, could never have those nice short cakes; but by using, or calling up this common sense, and reasoning a little, they may say, 'now I have not got the oatmeal, nor can I get it; but I will take milk in its place; and even, if no milk, I will take water, and by adding a little butter, lard or drippings, I will have just as good a cake' – and so they would. Now, please judge, in the same manner, in all cases, where such difficulties may of necessity arise, then these remarks will have their intended effect. I will add this word, only, additional, those who don't know anything more than simply to always confine themselves to, or follow a recipe, or receipt, as generally called, (never changing it at all) will never amount to much, to themselves, or to the world. The above recipe says 'pumpkin, or squash' – everybody ought to know that squash will make the richer cake.

**Apple Shortcake** – Season well stewed apple sauce with sugar and nutmeg, or mace, make any of the nice shortcakes, above given, open, or split, as the case may be, butter nicely and spread on a thick layer of the prepared sauce, and replace the top; serve with well sweetened cream.

*Remarks* – You will need to have quite a quantity, if you satisfy the taste and desires of the family, and the guests. The following from dried apples, will enable families to have apple shortcake all the year round, says a writer in the New York *Post*.

**Apple Shortcake From Dried Apples** – I will tell you of something that makes an agreeable filling for a shortcake. You will not believe it until you try it, but for those unfortunate ones to whom the acid of the strawberry is as poison, it can not be too highly recommended. Take some nice dried apples, wash and soak, and cook them until they are tender; then rub them through a sieve or a fine colander, add sugar and the grated rind and juice of a lemon; then make a shortcake in the ordinary manner and use this in place of the berries.

The next five recipes I take from the New York *Tribune*, headed 'Some Southern Recipes,' which will prove valuable to some people, no doubt, in the North as well as in the South, and as they are all in the nature of biscuit or cakes, except the last one – 'Velvet Cream,' – I will keep them together as found in the *Tribune*.

1. **Southern Biscuit** – Two cups of self-rising flour, 1 spoonful of lard; mix with warm milk; knead into soft dough, and roll; cut with a biscuit cutter and prick each with a straw. Cook in a hot oven 10 minutes.

2. **Palmetto Flannel Cakes** – One pt. of buttermilk, 2 well-beaten eggs, flour enough to make a stiff batter – the flour to be mixed, half wheat and half corn flour. Put a tea-spoonful of sea foam into the flour and cook on a griddle.

3. **Breakfast Muffins** – For a small family, use 1 pt. of milk, 3 gills of wheat flour, 3 eggs, and a pinch of salt. Beat the eggs very light, add the milk, and lastly stir in the flour. Bake in rings or small pans and in a quick oven. They are very light.

4. **Breakfast Waffles** – After breakfast stir into the hominy that is left 1 tea-spoonful of butter and a little salt. Set it aside. The next morning thin it with milk and add 2 eggs, beaten well. Stir in flour enough to make the right consistency, and bake in waffle-irons.

5. **Velvet Cream** – Two table-spoonfuls of gelatine, dissolved in ½ a tumbler of water; 1 pt. of rich cream, 4 table-spoonfuls of sugar; flavor with sherry, vanilla extract, or rose water. This is a delicious dessert, and can

be made in a few minutes. It may be served with or without cream.

**Muffins, No. 1, Very Light and Nice** – Flour, sifted, 1 qt.; sugar, 1 cup; eggs, 1; sweet milk, 2 cups; lard, 1 heaping table-spoonful; salt, 1 tea-spoonful; baking powder, 2 tea-spoonfuls. Mix on general principles; put into muffin rings, set in a pan, or, what is better, cast-iron muffin rings made in sets, and hot when dipped in, and placed at once into a quick oven. – *Mrs. Catharine Baldwin, Toledo, O.*

*Remarks* – This amount will make about 1½ dozen, so you can judge by the size of the family to use more or less material, as needed. Eaten in place of bread, with the meat course, then with butter and syrup, they are splendid. I think the nicest I ever ate. Very nice also cold. Although they are so light and dry, I do not object to eating them hot.

**Graham Gems** – I have been watching your papers to see if they gave any recipe for graham gems as good as mine. I have seen none. Take 1½ good pt. of graham flour, 1 pt. of sweet milk, mix them well together, beat the whites of 2 large eggs to a stiff foam, add yolks, beat well, heat gem pans hot, grease, have oven pretty hot, mix eggs in the last thing, carefully and quickly, as soon as they are beaten. Bake from 7 to 10 minutes. – *Mrs. M. P. Bush, Saline, Mich., in Detroit Post and Tribune.*

**Doughnuts, as Made by 'Peggy Shortcake'** – Sugar, 1 cup; 1 egg; sour milk, 1 cup; soda, ½ tea-spoonful; flour to mix as for biscuit. DIRECTIONS – 'Peggy' says: 'Roll pretty thin; have your lard boiling hot, and fry a nice brown. No dyspepsia about these; try 'em, if you want such as grow "way down East."'

**Fritters, Plain – Quick –** Sweet milk, 1 pt.; 4 eggs; salt, 1 tea-spoonful; baking powder, 1 table-spoonful; flour. DIRECTIONS – Beat the eggs well, stir in salt and milk; then put the baking powder into 2 or 3 cups of flour and stir in, using as much more flour as will stir in well; drop into hot lard. To be eaten with maple syrup, or syrup made by dissolving granulated sugar.

*Remarks –* 'Ivy,' of West Jefferson, Ohio, calls these Johnny Jumpup Cakes, because they jump up from the bottom of the hot lard so quickly and lightly.

**Buckwheat Griddle Cakes, in Rhyme –** For ordinary buckwheat cakes, we will give one in rhyme, from one of the muses of the Detroit *Free Press*, which may be relied upon as safe to follow:

> If you fine buckwheat cakes would make
> One quart of buckwheat flour take;
> Four table-spoonfuls then of yeast;
> Of salt one tea-spoonful at least;
> One handful Indian meal and two
> Good table-spoonfuls of real New
> Orleans molasses, then enough
> Warm water to make of the stuff
> A batter thin. Beat very well;
> Set it to rise where warmth do dwell.

If in the morning, it should be
The least bit sour, stir in free
A very little soda that
Is first dissolved in water hot.
Mix in an earthen crock, and leave
Each morn a cupful in to give
A sponge for the next night, so you
Need not get fresh yeast to renew.

In weather cold this plan may be
Pursued ten days successfully,
Providing you add every night
Flour, salt, molasses, meal in right
Proportions, beating as before,
And setting it to rise once more.
When baking make of generous size
Your cakes; and if they'd take the prize
They must be light and nicely browned,
Then by your husband you'll be crowned
Queen of the kitchen; but you'll bake,
And he will, man-like, 'take the cake.'

*Remarks* – When buckwheat cakes are made without molasses, as is often done, if a small spoonful of molasses is added, each morning, to the cake batter, they will take a much nicer brown, being careful, however, not to burn them.

# VARIOUS DISHES

**Meat Loaf, from Beef, Veal, Mutton, or Ham, Left Over** – Chop fine all such meats as you have left over from previous meals, fat and lean together, with a chopped onion, if allowable; a few slices of dry bread which have been soaked in milk, pressing out the superfluous milk; an egg for each person, and mix all together with pepper and salt as needed. Make into a loaf and bake nicely for breakfast or tea. Mashed potatoes, or fried, sliced from raw ones, are very nice with this relish.

**Ham Cakes, Baked, for Breakfast or Tea** – Take the remnants of a boiled ham, fat and lean together. Chop fine, and pound with a steak-pounder, or, if you have one, run it through a sausage machine. Soak a large piece of bread for each person to be served in milk; a beaten egg, also, for each person, a little pepper, and all mixed together, put into a suitable pudding dish and bake a nice brown. Call this ham pudding if you prefer. It will pass for either.

**OATMEAL** – For Bone and Muscle; or, as Food and Drink for Laborers – Liebig has shown that oatmeal is almost as nutritious as the very best English beef, and that it is richer than wheaten bread in the elements that go to form bone and muscle. Prof. Forbes, of Edinburgh, during some 20 years, measured the breadth and height, and also tested the strength of both the arms and loins of the students of the University – a very numerous class, and of various nationalities, drawn to Edinburgh by the fame of his teaching. He found that in height, breadth of chest and shoulders, and strength of arms and loins, the Belgians were at the bottom of the list, a little above them the French, very much higher the English, and highest of all the Scotch and Scotch-Irish, from Ulster, who, like the natives of Scotland, are fed in their early years with at least one meal a day of good milk and good oatmeal porridge.

**As a Drink** – Speaking of oatmeal an exchange remarks that a very good drink is made by putting about 2 spoonfuls of the meal into a tumbler of water. The western hunters and trappers consider it the best of drinks, as it is at once nourishing, stimulating and satisfying. It is popular in the Brooklyn navy yard, 2½ lbs. of oatmeal being put into a pail of moderately cold water. It is much better than any of the ordinary mixtures of vinegar and molasses with water, which farmers use in the haying and harvest field. – *New York Mail*.

*Remarks* – I know the value of oatmeal as a food; and I have not a doubt of its value as a drink; putting the meal to common water for the drinking, by laborers, when at work. My son and myself drank of it, as used by the laborers on the Brooklyn bridge, as we visited that structure, passing through there to the Centennial in 1876, and liked it very much; and the superintendent said he should not be willing to even try to do without it; though I think they only put 1 lb. to a pail of water. It would certainly be very nourishing with 2 table-spoonfuls of it to a glass of water, as spoken of by the exchange

69

above; half the amount would meet my own ideas, as sufficient, even when the nourishment was especially needed.

**Potato Fritters** – This receipt was given by one of those persons who more recently have been having schools of instruction in the cities in the art of cookery, Miss Parloa. She says:

One pint of boiled and mashed potato; ½ cup of hot milk; 3 table-spoonfuls of butter; 3 of sugar; 2 eggs; a little nutmeg; 1 tea-spoonful of salt. DIRECTIONS – Add the milk, butter, sugar and seasoning to the mashed potato, and then add the eggs well beaten. Stir until very smooth and light. Spread about ½ an inch deep on a buttered dish, and set away to cool. When cold, cut into squares. Dip in beaten egg and in bread-crumbs, and fry brown, in boiling fat. Serve immediately.

*Remarks* – I take this to be only another name for potato balls, but they will be a nice thing to have around about mealtime.

**Sweet Potato Cakes – Very Nice** – Remove the skin from 2 or 3 medium-sized sweet potatoes, left over, and mash them nicely, and mix in about 3 ozs. (3 small table-spoonfuls) of flour, salt and pepper to taste, a good lump of butter, and warm milk enough to make a good dough. Roll this out on the kneading board, and cut out a cake about the size of your baking tin; butter the tin well, and scatter a little flour over it; then lay in; when you think it is nearly done, turn it over. If the bottom of the oven is very hot, put a grate under the baking-tin to prevent getting too much browned. The danger of burning is lessened if instead of one cake you cut the dough in biscuit-shape about 2 inches thick. If covered while baking, the cakes will be more moist. These can be made of other potatoes as well as of the sweet ones.

*Remarks* – Either of these plans not only enable one to use up cold or leftover sweet potatoes, but 'Irish' potatoes, too, and at the same time make a nice dish for the table – the same as though the potatoes had been cooked purposely for these uses; in fact, it is well to cook some extra ones for either of these purposes, preferred, at the time.

**Pumpkin Butter, as Made in the North Woods** – Take out the seeds of 1 pumpkin, cut it in small pieces and boil it soft; take 3 other pumpkins, cut them in pieces and boil them soft; put them in a coarse bag and press out the juice; add the juice to the first pumpkin and let it boil 10 hours or more to become the thickness of butter; stir often. If the pumpkins are frozen the juice will come out much easier.

*Remarks* – All I have to guide me as to the 'North Woods' manner of making is that on the back of the slip cut from some newspaper, there was the date of the paper – Feb. 7, 1880, – also 'Sleighing fair,' and 'Loggers feel better;' therefore, to know that 'loggers felt better,' they must have that class of persons among them; and hence it was from some northern paper, where loggers in the winter do congregate. It will make a good butter if boiled carefully to avoid burning. I should say boil the juice at least half away before putting in the nicely cut pieces of the 1 pumpkin, boiling it soft in the juice of the 3 other ones, after its reduction one-half. It makes a very good substitute for cow's butter, and for apple butter, too. But I must say if I used frozen pumpkins to obtain the juice from, I should not want the one frozen that was to be cut up to make the butter of. I think it would not be as good if frozen. If any of these butters are too sour add good brown sugar to make it sweet enough to suit the taste.

**Frosted Figs for Dessert** – Beat the whites of 2, 3 or more eggs, according to the amount you wish to serve, till so stiff you can almost turn the plate upside down without the egg running off; then stir in powdered sugar, to leave the frosting soft enough to dip the figs into it, to completely cover, if need be, by re-dipping. Dry in the oven or on a shelf above the stove. If done nicely they will be nice.

**Boston Cream Toast** – Cut stale bread in slices ¼ inch thick, and toast a nice light chestnut color. Put 1 pt. of milk to heat with ½ cup of butter, a little pepper, and salt to suit the taste. Blend 2 large tea-spoonfuls of flour with cold milk, and when it boils, stir in and let it boil 2 or 3 minutes. – Now have ready a pan of hot water, a little salted, dip each slice quickly in the water, lay in a hot dish and cover with the hot cream. Serve immediately.

II. Another nice dish is made by rolling light bread dough thin, cutting in strips and boiling in hot fat. Break each cake open as it comes from the kettle, and plunge it into the above cream.

*Remarks* – As Boston claims to be the 'hub' upon which the world turns, I have thought to close the toast making with the Bostonian plan of making cream toast, as given by 'P.' of Toledo. It will be found very nice, and the second dish, or plan, using the same cream, will undoubtedly suit many persons – try them both, if fond of nice dishes.

**Piccalilli, A Good Substitute for Sauces** – Green tomatoes, 1 pk.; 1 large cabbage; 1 dozen onions; chop them fine and put on ½ pt. of salt and let them stand over night; then drain off the brine, and scald in weak vinegar and drain off again; and now add 6 good-sized green peppers chopped fine, having removed the seeds before chopping; ½ to 1 pt. (as you like best) of grated horseradish; then season with ground spices to suit the taste, at least 1 table-spoonful of allspice and pepper, and half as much dry mustard; and also ½ table-spoonful of cloves. Now, in packing in a jar, if 6 to 8 or 10 quite small cucumbers (whole), which have stood in salt and water over night, are put upon each layer of an inch or two in thickness, they will be found a valuable addition, putting one in each sauce dish when served at table. Then all being closely packed, just cover with good vinegar, boiling hot, and cover closely, or put up in fruit jars, if plenty, and you will have a dish, as the saying is, 'nice enough for a king;' the author says nice enough for a better man than a king – nice enough for 'an American citizen.'

# *In Memoriam*

DR. ALVIN WOOD CHASE, physician, and author of the celebrated Dr. Chase's Receipt Book, was born in Cayuga County, New York, in 1817. He was a son of Benjamin Chase, a native of the State of Massachusetts. When Alvin was eleven years of age his parents located near Buffalo, N.Y., where he grew to manhood, receiving a very limited education, in a log school-house. His desire for knowledge was so strong, coupled with an ambition peculiar to his naturally energetic disposition, that he far outstripped his more dilatory companions of that humble institute of learning. When seventeen years old he left New York and found employment on the Maumee River, in the meantime devoting his spare moments to study. In 1840 he located at Dresden, Ohio, where in the spring of 1841 he married Martha Shutts, daughter of Henry and Martha Shutts, natives of New York. To this noble and gifted wife, and mother of his children, may be justly attributed much of the success that followed the doctor during his long and eventful career. From the days of his boyhood he entertained a wish to study medicine, and awaited with impatience the time when he might become a member of the fraternity. After many wanderings he settled in Ann Arbor, Mich., in 1856, where, to his intense delight, he was enabled vigorously to prosecute his studies in what was to be his future life-work.

He attended lectures in the medical department of the State University during 1857 and 1858, and graduated from the Eclectic Institute of Cincinnati, Ohio, in the meantime. Prior to 1869 he traveled over a large part of the United States, acquiring valuable knowledge, only gained by practical experience, which proved a good foundation for the wonderful book which afterward gained such great celebrity. The first edition of the work, like all subsequent ones, proved a great success, and soon placed the author on the high road to fortune. In 1864 he built the first part of that magnificent structure that still bears his name. It stands on the corner of Main Street and Miller Avenue, and is an ornament to our city. The building was completed in 1868. The business had so increased that at this time fifty persons found constant and remunerative employment within the walls of the building; and the hospitality and liberality of the Doctor to the employees of the institution, as well as to the needy ones of the city, were always subjects of admiring comment.

In 1873 he published his second book, of which many thousand copies were sold, and it is safe to say that fully one million and a half have found their way into the homes of this and foreign countries.

A few years only have elapsed since Dr. Chase was considered one of the most prosperous and well-to-do citizens of Ann Arbor; losses by thousands and tens of thousands of dollars greatly reduced his accumulations so honestly acquired. It is seldom the case that so much wealth is secured in so short a time by honest endeavor. He entered into no speculating schemes, but industriously pursued a very useful calling, bringing large profits without detriment to any, but, on the contrary, of great value to all. But, notwithstanding his losses, he did not lose his native energy and manliness of purpose, and stood before the community a conspicuous example of what energy, perseverance, and an indomitable will may accomplish. He was long connected with the Methodist church at Ann Arbor, to which, from time to time, he donated large sums of money. His liberality in this direction was remarkable, considering his income, though large. Many men, whose means were quadruple those of the Doctor, did not give one quarter as much for the advancement of this and other benevolent enterprises.

He was once nominated for mayor of the city, but his business compelled him to decline the proffered honor. But the storms of life finally overtook him and swept with almost resistless fury around the now aged physician, and a few of the prejudices that characterize the human family found a resting place in the heart of this noble man; yet, when the last chapter shall have been entered in the book of life, the account will probably be balanced. The last earthly rites have been performed, and the aged veteran laid peacefully away beneath the shadow of the silent tomb. It may truthfully be said that he lived with malice toward none and charity to all. A beautiful monument marks the place where his earthly remains are laid away, but his real and ever-enduring monument is seen in his life, devotion and usefulness to his fellow man.

Rev. L. Davis,
*Secretary of the Washtenaw County
Pioneer Society.*

Ann Arbor, Nov. 28, 1886.

## FROM ABSINTHE TO ZEST
### *An Alphabet for Food Lovers*

*Alexandre Dumas*

AS WELL AS BEING THE AUTHOR OF *The Three Musketeers*, Alexandre Dumas was also an enthusiastic gourmand and expert cook. His *Grand Dictionnaire de Cuisine*, published in 1873, is an encyclopaedic collection of ingredients, recipes and anecdotes, from Absinthe to Zest via cake, frogs' legs, oysters, roquefort and vanilla.

Included here are recipes for bamboo pickle and strawberry omelette, advice on cooking all manner of beast from bear to kangaroo – as well as delightful digressions into how a fig started a war and whether truffles really increase ardour – brought together in a witty and gloriously eccentric culinary compendium.

*'From the great French novelist and obsessive gourmet. The cook book as literature'*
NORMAN SPINRAD

# GREAT FOOD

## THE CAMPAIGN FOR DOMESTIC HAPPINESS

*Isabella Beeton*

FIRMLY OF THE BELIEF THAT A HOME should be run as an efficient military campaign, Mrs Beeton, the doyenne of English cookery, offers timeless tips on selecting cuts of meat, throwing a grand party and hosting a dinner, as well as giving suggestions on staff wages and the cost of each recipe.

With such delicious English classics as rabbit pie, carrot soup, baked apple custard, and fresh lemonade – as well as invalid's jelly for those days when stewed eels may be a little too much – this is a wonderful collection of food writing from the matriarch of modern housekeeping.

*'Sublime . . . A Victorian gem'*
JULIAN BARNES

····· GREAT FOOD ·····

## THE JOYS OF EXCESS

*Samuel Pepys*

AS WELL AS BEING THE MOST celebrated
diarist of all time, Samuel Pepys was also a hearty
drinker, eater and connoisseur of epicurean
delights, who indulged in every pleasure
seventeenth-century London had to offer.

Whether he is feasting on barrels of oysters,
braces of carps, larks' tongues and copious amounts
of wine, merrymaking in taverns until the early
hours, attending formal dinners with lords and ladies
or entertaining guests at home with his young wife,
these irresistible selections from Pepys's diaries
provide a frank, high-spirited and vivid picture
of the joys of over-indulgence – and the
side-effects afterwards.

*'Vigorous, precise, enchanting . . . the most ordinary and
the most extraordinary writer you will ever meet'*
CLAIRE TOMALIN

GREAT FOOD

## A LITTLE DINNER
## BEFORE THE PLAY

*Agnes Jekyll*

WHETHER EXTOLLING THE MERITS of a cheerful
breakfast tray, conjuring up a winter picnic of figs and mulled
wine, sharing delicious Tuscan recipes, or suggesting a
last-minute pre-theatre dinner, the sparkling writings of the
society hostess and philanthropist Agnes Jekyll describe food
for every imaginable occasion and mood.

Originally published in *The Times* in the early 1920s,
these divinely witty and brilliantly observed pieces are
still loved today for their warmth and friendly advice
and, with their emphasis on fresh, simple, stylish dishes,
were years ahead of their time.

*'Beautifully written, sparkling, witty and knowing,*
*an absolute delight to read'*
INDIA KNIGHT

GREAT FOOD

## A DISSERTATION UPON ROAST PIG & OTHER ESSAYS

*Charles Lamb*

A RAPTUROUS APPRECIATION of pork crackling, a touching description of hungry London chimney sweeps, a discussion of the strange pleasure of eating pineapple and a meditation on the delights of Christmas feasting are just some of the subjects of these personal, playful writings from early nineteenth-century essayist Charles Lamb.

Exploring the joys of food and also our complicated social relationship with it, these essays are by turns sensuous, mischievous, lyrical and self-mocking. Filled with a sense of hunger, they are some of the most fascinating and nuanced works ever written about eating, drinking and appetite.

*'The Georgian essayist, tender and puckish, with a weakness for oddity and alcohol, is one of the great chroniclers of London'*
OBSERVER

GREAT FOOD

## THE WELL-KEPT KITCHEN
*Gervase Markham*

IN 1615 THE POET AND WRITER Gervase
Markham published an extraordinary handbook
for housewives, containing advice on everything
from planting herbs to brewing beer, feeding animals
to distilling perfume, with recipes for a variety of
dishes such as trifle, pancakes and salads (not to
mention some amusingly tart words on how the
ideal wife should behave).

Aimed at middle-class women who would share
in household tasks with their servants in the kitchen,
this companionable and opinionated book offers a
richly enjoyable glimpse of the way we lived,
worked and ate 400 years ago.

······ GREAT FOOD ······

## RECIPES FROM
## THE WHITE HART INN
*William Verrall*

WILLIAM VERRALL, the redoubtable eighteenth-century landlord of the White Hart Inn in Lewes, Sussex, trained under a continental chef and was determined to introduce the 'modern and best French cookery' to his customers. Gently mocking Englishmen who eat plain mutton chops or only possess one frying-pan, he gives enthusiastic advice on must-have kitchen gadgets and describes enticing dishes such as truffles in French wine and mackerel with fennel.

This selection also includes the recipes that the poet Thomas Gray scribbled in his own well-thumbed copy of Verrall's *Complete System of Cookery*, which was one of the best-loved food books of its time.

'Racily written'
ALAN DAVIDSON